The Complete Screenwriter's Manual

The Complete Screenwriter's Manual

A Comprehensive Reference of Format and Style

Stephen E. Bowles
University of Miami

Ronald Mangravite
University of Miami

Peter A. Zorn, Jr.
Screenwriter

PEARSON

Boston   New York   San Francisco
Mexico City   Montreal   Toronto   London   Madrid   Munich   Paris
Hong Kong   Singapore   Tokyo   Cape Town   Sydney

Senior Editor: Molly Taylor
Editorial Assistant: Suzanne Stradley
Manufacturing Buyernne Sweeney
Design: Carol Somberg
Cover Designer: Kristina Mose-Libon

For related titles and support materials, visit our online catalog at www.ablongman.com.

ISBN: 0-321-39793-2

Printed in the United States of America

10 9 8 7 6 5 4   10   09   08   07

Contents

It's an incredibly difficult business. You can have great ideas, you can have all the talent in the world, but you have to get lucky. And no one has the formula for luck. The only consolation to this is that once you get lucky, you look different and then it gets easier.

From the novel *The Player*
By Michael Tolkin

Preface
WHY WE WROTE THIS BOOK

The craft of screenwriting essentially comes down to two questions: What is the story I want to tell? and How can I best write that story in screenplay format?

All screenwriters, from the absolute beginner to the Oscar-winning professional, must face these questions each and every time they sit down to write.

Most books on screenwriting focus only on the first question. There are scores, perhaps hundreds of how-to texts about plot structure, character development, and dramatic fundamentals. Many of these books provide excellent advice and tools for story construction.

The second question is more elusive. A few workbooks offer the basics of traditional screenplay format rules. Most of these contain standard screenplay templates but offer little help in *how* to use them effectively or even *why* the rules are there.

And very, very few screenwriting books concentrate on the essential task of how to translate the story from the writer's imagination to the pages of a screenplay. No book that we know of provides a complete reference for writers who are faced with specific format and style situations.

We come to this project having worn many hats—produced screenwriter, writing instructor, development executive, story analyst, producer, and director. Among the three of us, we have read thousands of screenplays and teleplays. We have examined both how screenplay format and style have evolved from the early studio days to the present and what trends are current in today's competitive marketplace.

Steve Bowles
Ron Mangravite
Peter Zorn

HOW WILLIAM GOLDMAN LEARNED TO WRITE A SCREENPLAY

We talked for a few minutes more all very calmly until suddenly it hit me—I didn't know what the hell a screenplay looked like!

Madness.

I tore down to Times Square, where there was an all-night bookstore. There aren't shelves full of books on screenwriting even now, but back then, what we have today seems like a gusher. I nervously asked the clerk did he have any books on what a screenplay looked like and he sort of nervously waved me back in the general direction of the rear of the place. *Everyone* was nervous in Times Square at two in the morning, then and now, in bookstores or on the streets. The other few customers eyed me strangely and I suppose I gave as good as I got. God knows what they were doing there, pushing, dozing, maybe bookworms with insomnia or other budding screenwriters; they went their way, I mine. I don't know how long I took, but there was one copy of one book with the word *screenwriting* in the title so I grabbed it, blew away (truly) the dust, clocked the contents table, flicked through until I finally got to the pages that showed what a screenplay looked like.

More madness.

To this day I remember staring at the page in shock. I didn't know what it was exactly I was looking at, but I knew I could never write in that form, in that language.

> Novelist and screenwriter, William Goldman
> From *Adventures in the Screen Trade:*
> *A Personal View of Hollywood and*
> *Screenwriting* (1983)

HOW LARRY McMURTRY LEARNED TO WRITE A SCREENPLAY

Finally, though, in a bookshop on Hollywood Boulevard, I was able to purchase (for $40) a Xeroxed copy of the script of *Hud*, and got to see what one of the things looked like. Shortly thereafter, my education took a great leap forward when Peter Bogdanovich hired me to collaborate with him on the screenplay for my third novel, *The Last Picture Show*. At this point I was still so ignorant of film mechanics that I supposed the only way to get from one scene to the next was by means of a cut. My initial step-sheet for *The Last Picture Show* offered the director an unbroken sequence of quick cuts. Peter and his then wife, Polly Platt, were wildly amused by this; the walls of their modest bungalow in Van Nuys veritably shook from their laughter. Unfortunately, in their hilarity, they forgot to explain to me what the other modes of transition were, and to this day most of the technical information I possess about the making of movies has been picked up through eavesdropping at luncheon conversations in various studio commissaries.

> Novelist and screenwriter, Larry McMurtry
> From *Film Flam: Essays on Hollywood*
> (1987)

Acknowledgments

The authors wish to express their thanks to the following for their support:

Sam L. Grogg
Dean, American Film Institute Conservatory

Paul Lazarus
Director, Motion Picture Program, University of Miami
School of Communication

Denise Mann
Co-Chair, Producers Program, UCLA Dept. of Film/TV

Paul Nagel, Jr.
Professor Emeritus, Motion Pictures Program, University of Miami
School of Communication

Edward Pfister
Dean, University of Miami School of Communication

David Schroeder
Miami-Dade College

Richard Walter
Chair, Screenwriting Program, UCLA Dept. of Film/TV

The following reviewers provided helpful comments on the text:

Lou Buttino
University of North Carolina, Wilmington

Edward F. Emanuel
California State University, Fresno

Allan Havis
University of California, San Diego

Terry McAteer
Felician College

Barry Russal
Palm Beach Community College

David Wesner
Austin Peay State University

Introduction

The Complete Screenwriter's Manual offers a clear, direct, and concise guide to the complex process of formatting ideas for motion picture screenplays. It provides a learning approach to understanding and mastering the form in which screenplays must be written for today's competitive market.

Eventually, you will discard the learning aspects of the manual and use it as a reference.

Two important points need to be understood before using this manual.

First, *The Complete Screenwriter's Manual* is designed for the novice screenwriter who has little or no experience writing in the required format.

- The professional screenwriter will already have a working knowledge of this process and be well beyond the parameters of a manual such as this one.

- Further, a professional screenwriter will have tweaked the basic format to fit his or her own stylistic preferences and may well argue with some of the techniques described. But even the seasoned professional must adhere to the fundamental conventions.

Second, *The Complete Screenwriter's Manual* presents *a way* to format screenplays.

- There is no one-and-only way. This manual provides a clean and safe way to use the format. If you pick up ten professional screenplays at random, you will likely find ten variations. Although each will adhere to the fundamental conventions, each will have minor stylistic differences.

- The look of the page is extremely important because it is what the reader first sees. You want to make a good first impression.

- Screenwriting professionals and teachers will disagree about the details of the format. Arguments over such matters as the application of transitions or the definition of a slug line will not substantively affect the format.

At this stage of your screenwriting experience, these issues are minor. What is important is mastering the *basic concepts* of the format. After that, there is room for flexibility.

How to Use This Book

Every effort has been made to present the process of formatting a screenplay in a simple and reasonable way. This is accomplished by providing a step-by-step approach, moving from the most fundamental elements to the more complex.

The manual is divided into four parts:

Part One: Basic Format and Style contains the essential elements that you will use on every page of every script.

Part Two: Advanced Format and Style provides techniques that will enhance your storytelling skills.

Part Three: Special Format Situations explains specific screenwriting situations that are more complicated.

Part Four: Common Format Mistakes contains examples of the most frequently observed errors in screenwriting format.

On Screenplay Format and Style

TRADITIONAL SCREENWRITING

Screenplay format has evolved from the heyday of the Hollywood studio system in the first half of the twentieth century. At that time, scripts were written by writers under contract to the studios, and they were usually written for specific stars, who were also under studio contract. The story concepts, whether adapted from other sources or original ideas, were usually approved by studio executives well before the scripts were ever written.

Studio screenwriters wrote in a standard format because this allowed the studio to effectively organize the production of a film, which was usually shot on the studio lot. The production concerns were basic: Is the scene an interior or an exterior? Does it take place during the day or night? What special props or effects does the scene require? What characters are in the scene and in what costumes? In addition to telling a story, the screenplay was the equivalent of a contractor's blueprint, a device to organize the production and utilize the expertise of others.

The studio system, as a dominant channel of production, has all but disappeared. Now, most screenplays are created long before a production company gives a "green light" to produce it. But the production-based screenplay remains. In Part One, you will learn the basic elements of screenplay format.

CONTEMPORARY SCREENWRITING

Today's screenplays are most often written before any stars, directors, or financiers are attached to the project and before a studio agrees to market and distribute the picture. This situation has brought big changes in the function of screenplay format. Screenplays are now used to persuade everyone in the Hollywood "food chain"—producers, directors, actors, executives, and script readers—that the project *must* be made. Therefore, screenplays today are geared to attract and entice the talent and funding required to make the movie.

The screenplay is now a deal-making device. As such, it must be more dynamic, colorful, and vital than what was required in the past. For the screenwriter, this means applying advanced format and stylistic techniques to enhance "the read." This will be the focus of Part Two.

About Screenplay Software

Most professional screenwriters use screenwriting software, which offers the convenience of automatically formatted margins, page numbering, and other time-saving features. But while such software is convenient to use, it does not eliminate the need to understand and master the basics of screenplay format and style. Also, most format and style applications, from character descriptions to slug lines, are far beyond the scope of software.

Dozens of software programs are available today, but three dominate the market. All are easy to use, offer a wide range of useful features, and have good tech support.

- *Final Draft* has been the acknowledged leader in the entertainment industry for many years. It includes twelve script formats (including several television script formats) and provides tech support.

- *Movie Magic Screenwriter* is less entrenched as an industry leader but has more features, including free tech support.

- *Scriptware* is also very good. It is very simple to use and is touted as the most popular screenwriting software in the world.

Prices for these programs vary widely, from a high of nearly $300 to a low of around $100. All three are readily available online.

One ultra low-cost alternative is *Hollywood Screenwriter,* essentially a stripped down version of *Movie Magic.* While this bare-bones program lacks the advanced features and conveniences of the leading software programs, it is perfectly useful.

Screenwriting software can be very helpful but is not essential. All the basic functions of screenwriting format can be achieved by using a basic word-processing program, such as *Microsoft Word* or *Word Perfect.*

Assumptions about the Reader of a Screenplay

Because of the large number of scripts that are submitted, script readers—usually professionals hired by agents, producers, and executives—will give a screenplay only cursory attention, at least initially. Therefore, if a screenplay is to have a chance of proceeding further, the writer must work on certain assumptions:

- A screenplay will probably be read *once* and read *quickly.*

- Most readers will form an initial perception of a screenplay on the basis of the *first 10 or so pages.* These pages, therefore, must "grab" the reader and encourage further reading.

- The reader needs to be satisfied that everything in a screenplay has a *purpose* and corresponding *meaning;* nothing should be gratuitous.

The screenplay is very literal and is to be written and read *as the movie would unfold*. The key to writing a screenplay, therefore, is to translate the sights and sounds of a movie from your imagination to the written word as it appears on the page.

- Screenwriting is not about having great language skills. Rather it is about having great story and character skills. The prose should therefore avoid poetic descriptions, inflated vocabulary, and complex syntax.

Because a screenplay is designed to attract talent for a production, what is more important than writing a masterwork of literature is to write a script that is *clear* and *direct*, always allowing the narrative and characters to determine and dominate the writing.

Gaining the Reader's Confidence

If your screenplay looks sloppy or is improperly formatted or if it contains inconsistencies or misspellings, then the reader will lose confidence in you and your screenplay.

- Create a good master copy, preferably from a laser printer, and use a quality photocopying process to make duplicates.

- Use a fresh, clean copy for each new submission. You do not want to give the impression that you are re-circulating the same pages that others have read (and perhaps rejected).

  For this reason, it is a poor practice to put a date on a screenplay.

Treat each reader as if he or she is the first person to read your screenplay.

The Complete Screenwriter's Manual

PART ONE

Basic Format and Style

I read the first fifteen pages [of a screenplay] and, if it grabs me, I read the last fifteen pages. If nothing's changed, there's no point in reading the other hundred pages.

Michael Caine
Primetime, ABC Television (22 March 1990)

GUIDES TO THE APPEARANCE OF THE SCREENPLAY

Professional screenplays must conform to certain format rules.

- The typical **length** of a feature screenplay is 110 pages ($\pm$ 10 pages), on standard $8\frac{1}{2}" \times 11"$ plain white paper. Screenplays that exceed 120 pages or fall below 100 are generally disregarded by industry readers. Strive for 100 to 120 pages.

  The pages of a screenplay are traditionally printed only on one side. When a screenplay is read, the printed text is on the right-hand page and the left-hand page is blank. This convention was established to allow for re-write pages to be inserted into the script.

  NOTE:

  Sometimes scripts are printed on both sides of a page for reasons of economy and ecology. This non-standard practice is the case for certain talent agencies and production companies. We do not recommend that you follow this practice, as most professional readers strongly dislike two-sided script pages, which are harder to handle and lack space for notes. Also, the reduced thickness of a double-sided feature script makes it easily mistaken for a much shorter television episodic script.

- The current custom is for a screenplay to be delivered as **hard copy** only, not on a CD or in a web or e-mail file.

  Screenplays are submitted on three-hole-punched paper. The entire script, including the title page, is bound with brass brads or screw posts in the top and bottom holes only.

  A plain cardstock cover sheet may be used to protect the script. This cover sheet should have no writing or graphics.

- The conventional font for a screenplay is **12-point Courier** with non-justified right margins. Why the Courier font? There are two reasons:

  First, the accepted gauge that one page of screenplay approximates one minute of screen time is based on this customary layout. This measure would not work if you use, for example, a proportional font or a different point size or justify the margins.

  Second, psychologically, the use of Courier provides a more friendly and fluid appearance than would be the case if the screenplay appeared to be set in type as a published document. It is the difference between treating the screenplay as a "work in progress" rather than a "completed manuscript."

- Be sure to use standard American English spelling.

- The psychology of appearance of the screenplay cannot be over-emphasized. How it looks is half the struggle in getting it read.

The format is the vehicle by which the narrative is presented. Once mastered, the format should become second nature—the natural and fluid means through which your story is told.

SAMPLE SCREENPLAY PAGES

What follows are the first pages of *Aftershock*, an original feature-length screenplay.

You should read these pages before continuing with Part One. The format examples found later in Part One come from these pages. It will be useful to refer back to the *Aftershock* pages to see the examples in their proper context.

AFTERSHOCK

FADE IN:

INT.   TELEPHONE RELAY STATION - NIGHT

WARNER EVANS, late twenties, intense, handsome with closely
cropped hair and a neatly trimmed moustache, is working with
cool precision at one of the hundreds of banks of wiring
terminals. He is dressed in coveralls and wearing thin
latex gloves.

He reaches into his toolbox and removes a plastic case
containing a printed circuit board. He removes the board
from the case and, in order to keep his hands free, holds
the board gently in his mouth.

He removes a half-dozen sets of colored jumper cables and
sorts them between the fingers of one hand. Carefully, he
places a yellow jumper cable between two contacts, then a
blue one between two others, then another and another.

Once the cables are in place, he slowly removes a circuit
board from the panel. He takes the one from his mouth,
blows on the contacts to make sure they are clean and dry,
then slides it in place.

In the reverse order he removes all of the jumper cables
and carefully returns all the bits to the toolbox.

He pulls out a test handset and clips the wires at the end
of the coil cord to terminals on one of the panels. He
flips a switch and dials a number.

                    EVANS
                 (into handset)
          Harry? It's me, Warner. I'm supposed
          to meet Amanda and the Lewises, and I'm
          running late. Have they arrived yet?
                 (pause)
          That'll be fine. Thanks, Harry. Tell
          them I'm on my way.

He flips the switch again and disconnects the wires. He
returns the unit to the toolbox and closes it.

                                              CUT TO:

EXT.   TELEPHONE RELAY STATION - MINUTES LATER

Evans exits through a side door carrying his toolbox. He
walks close to the building, through a security gate and
out into the street.

                                          CUT TO:

EXT.   NEW ORLEANS STREET - CONTINUOUS

Evans walks half a block on the sidewalk, then crosses the
street to a bright yellow Lamborghini. He presses the alarm
button on his key ring and opens the passenger side door.

Placing the toolbox on the seat, he opens a white garbage
bag. He strips off the latex gloves and tosses them in the
bag. He then unzips the coveralls and wiggles out, revealing
a pleated white shirt with black bow tie.

He steps out of the legs and rolls the coveralls into a
ball. It follows the latex gloves into the garbage bag.

                                          CUT TO:

EXT.   DIFFERENT NEW ORLEANS STREET, A BRIDGE - LATER

The yellow Lamborghini moves swiftly along an empty wet
street. It slows to a stop close to the railing in the
middle of a long bridge. The passenger window rolls down.

SUDDENLY, the red toolbox sails out the window, over the
railing into the river below.

The window rolls up and the car slowly accelerates,
continuing over the bridge and down the empty street.

                                          CUT TO:

EXT.   A DESERTED ALLEY - CONTINUOUS

The Lamborghini enters the alley from the street and moves
slowly along. It stops next to a dumpster.

A DERELICT is sprawled on the ground in a half-seated position.
He props himself to a full sit and gestures to the yellow car.

Evans rolls down the window.

                    DERELICT
          Whoa. Ain't we the high and mighty with
          our pretty yellow car?

Evans tosses the garbage bag with the gloves and coveralls towards the man and speeds off.

The Derelict retrieves the bag and starts to open it. He stares after the car as it turns out of the alley and off up the street.

                    DERELICT (cont'd)
          Idiot.

In the distance, LIGHTNING flashes.

                                        CUT TO:

EXT.   STREET IN FRONT OF HARRY'S CLUB - LATER

A light rain. The Lamborghini pulls to a stop in front of the entrance. A half-dozen WELL-DRESSED PATRONS are gathered by the door.

Evans steps out of the car and is greeted by the VALET.

                    VALET
          Good evening Mr. Evans. And, how long
          will we be staying tonight?

                    EVANS
          I don't know for sure, Johnny. Probably
          at least two hours.

Evans reaches into the car and grabs his tuxedo jacket. He shakes it lightly and slides into it, then proceeds to the entrance.

The Valet climbs into the yellow car and slowly drives off.

                                        CUT TO:

INT.   HARRY'S CLUB - CONTINUOUS

Evans walks through the door into a large crowded room. OTHER PATRONS are seated at dozens of tables on a raised perimeter around a polished aluminum dance floor. Their CHATTER is almost overwhelming.

The walls are covered with brightly colored sections of chain link fencing. Mellow JAZZ MUSIC in the background.

Evans encounters two or three FRIENDS on his way to a table as they AD LIB polite greetings.

He arrives at a table for four. Seated at the table is CINDY LEWIS, late twenties and very attractive, and her husband, JACK LEWIS. Both are dressed in evening clothes.

Also at the table is AMANDA RICHARDS, slightly younger than
the Lewises, drop-dead gorgeous, dressed in a black suit
with a ruffled shirt with a large neck scarf.

Evans leans over and kisses Amanda softly, then takes a
seat.

                    EVANS
                (to the group)
        Sorry I'm late. This round's on me.

                    JACK
        Stuck in that accident on the
        Pontchartrain Bridge?

                    EVANS
        That.
                (pointing to the front of
                his shirt)
        And these damned studs. You'd think
        someone would invent a shirt stud that
        didn't require four hands to install.

They all laugh. Amanda reaches over and checks the row of
studs on Evans's shirt. She adjusts his bow tie and gives
him a kiss.

                    CINDY
                (to Amanda and Evans)
        Well. You got us here. And all
        dressed up I might add. What gives?

                    EVANS
        Really? I thought you two called this
        meeting.

                    JACK
        Not bloody likely, sport. Come on.
        What's up?

Evans raps his fork lightly against his glass to call the
group to mock attention.

                    EVANS
                (looking at Amanda)
        Well. We've decided to bite the bullet
        and get married.

                    JACK
        Well, well, well.

                    CINDY
        I must say, it's about time.

All four raise their glasses in a toast. Cindy slides her
chair closer to Amanda.

                    CINDY (cont'd)
          So. Where's the ring?

Amanda reaches into her purse and produces an engagement
ring. She slides it proudly onto her finger and waves it
slowly in front of Cindy.

As the women admire the ring, Lewis slides his chair across
toward Evans.

                    JACK
               (discreetly)
          Way to go, man. She's a real prize.

                    EVANS
          Couldn't agree more.

They watch the women for a moment.

                    JACK
          You'll never guess who I heard from
          this afternoon.

Evans looks at Jack and shrugs his shoulders.

                    JACK (cont'd)
          Colin Pryce.

Evans searches his memory.

                    JACK (cont'd)
          Little Colin Pryce. The kid that was
          always getting beaten up when we were
          in high school.

                    EVANS
               (smiling)
          Couple of years behind us, right? What
          did we used to call him? Pryce . . .

                    JACK
               (interrupting)
          Tag.

                    EVANS
          Yes. "Pryce tag." I can't believe how
          stupid that sounds after all these years.
                    (MORE)

                              EVANS (CONT'D)
                    I guess he survived high school. What
                    ever became of him?

                              JACK
                    He was a little vague on that, but I get
                    the feeling he's with the FBI or
                    something. Maybe the CIA.

                              EVANS
                    Why does that not surprise me? Working
                    for an acronym seems to fit. What's he
                    here for? He's a far cry from Gary,
                    Indiana.

                              JACK
                    I suppose you could say the same thing
                    about us.

Evans laughs again. The women, noting this, return their
attention to the men.

                              AMANDA
                    What's so funny, you two?

                              EVANS
                    We're just talking about an old high
                    school classmate.

The WAITER comes to the table.

                                                          CUT TO:

INT.   FBI FIELD OFFICE - NIGHT

NOTE: This space is actually a makeshift office in a
warehouse, the kind of unit that can be loaded into a tractor
trailer and relocated at a moment's notice.

Three MALE AGENTS are working at a table in the corner,
comparing documents with data on one of the bulletin boards.

The large room is filled with temporary work units.
Computer and electrical cables are taped to the floor.
Large work tables and portable bulletin boards seem to be
everywhere.

Into the room walks COLIN PRYCE, mid twenties, short, red
haired wearing a moderately priced suit. He tosses his
raincoat on one of the cluttered tables and crosses to the
agents.

                              PRYCE
                    Okay, ladies. What have we got?

Pryce moves to the table and picks up a file folder. He
scans its contents.

                    AGENT ONE
          Not much. We're logging these phone
          records. Trying to match the times and
          places. It's pretty slow going.

                    PRYCE
          Keep on it, Larry.

Pryce returns to the table where he tossed his coat. He
clears a small work area. He picks up the phone and dials.

                    VOICE (V.O.)
               (over phone)
          Dallas Center.

                    PRYCE
               (into phone)
          Agent Phillip Barnes, please.

                    VOICE (V.O.)
               (over phone)
          One moment please.

Pryce sorts through one of the piles of papers in front of
him.

                    AGENT BARNES (V.O.)
               (over phone)
          Phil Barnes.

                    PRYCE
               (into phone)
          Phil. Colin Pryce, here.

                    AGENT BARNES (V.O.)
               (over phone)
          Hey . . . Colin. What's up?

                    PRYCE
               (into phone)
          I need everything you guys have in the
          201 on Operation MERCY. Send it on
          TRAN-6.

                    AGENT BARNES (V.O.)
               (over phone)
          That won't take long. The man's well
          covered. We haven't come up with
          anything criminal or even connected.
          He's clean as a whistle.

                    PRYCE
               (into phone)
          Same here. What gives with this guy?
          Who's he working for?

                    AGENT BARNES (V.O.)
               (over phone)
          Somebody higher than us, old buddy.
          Maybe CIA . . . or military.

                    PRYCE
               (into phone)
          Definitely not military. I went to
          high school with this guy and trust me,
          military is not an option. Send me
          whatever you've got. You never know
          what might surface.

                    AGENT BARNES (V.O.)
               (over phone)
          I'll get it right off. Good luck.
          Catch you later.

Pryce hangs up the phone and reaches to his shirt pocket.

Finding it empty, he gets up and crosses to his raincoat.
He reaches into the pocket and retrieves a pack of
cigarettes and a worn Zippo lighter.

He lights a cigarette and returns to the work table.

Agent One crosses to the table.

                    AGENT ONE
          Any luck?

                    PRYCE
               (irritated)
          Dallas says he's clean as a whistle.

                    AGENT ONE
          You know, Colin, there's no smoking in
          here.

Pryce SLAMS his fist against the table.

                    PRYCE
          New rule, son. There is now.

Agent One looks at him in disbelief.

                                        DISSOLVE TO:

INT. EVANS'S LIVING ROOM - MORNING

The large impeccably neat room has high ceilings and tall
windows taking full advantage of the morning light. One wall
has floor to ceiling book cases filled with leather-bound
volumes. Another has a large marble fireplace.

In the center of the room facing the fireplace is a large
tufted leather sofa. The coffee table is an old flat
drawing file with a glass top. It contains a collection of
Civil War pistols.

On the corner of the glass top is a single-edged razor blade
and a faint residue of WHITE POWDER.

Evans is sitting on the sofa having coffee and reading the
paper. There is a KNOCK at the front door.

Evans puts down the paper and goes to the door. He opens
it to find Colin Pryce standing on the front porch.

                    PRYCE
          Good morning, Warner. Remember me?

                    EVANS
          Colin Pryce. Come on in. What are you
          doing here?

Pryce enters the room and looks around in amazement as
Evans closes the door.

                    EVANS (cont'd)
          Can I get you a cup of coffee?

                    PRYCE
          That would be great.

Evans calls to the next room.

                    EVANS
          Charlie. Bring another cup, will you
          please?

                    CHARLIE (O.S.)
               (Jamaican accent)
          Soon be comin', Mon.

CHARLIE, a six-foot-tall black man with a wide smile, enters
the room carrying a silver tray with a cup and saucer. He
places it on the coffee table and leaves.

Evans pours a cup and hands it to Pryce. He motions for
him to sit.

                         EVANS
          So what brings you to rainy New
          Orleans?

Pryce takes a seat on the sofa across from Evans and sips
his coffee.

                         PRYCE
          Good coffee, thanks. I'm here for a
          few days on business.

                         EVANS
          Jack Lewis said you were in town.

                         PRYCE
          Called him yesterday. Tried to get
          you, but there was no answer. You
          don't have a machine?

                         EVANS
          Don't believe in them. No cell either.
          You either get me or call back.
                    (beat)
          So, what business are you in?

                         PRYCE
          Data gathering and interpretation
          mostly . . . a lot of travel.

The phone RINGS. Evans gets up and crosses to the desk.

                         EVANS
                    (sarcastic)
          See how it works. I'm here. The phone
          rings. I answer it.

Evans picks up the remote phone from its base unit.

                         EVANS (cont'd)
                    (into phone)
          Warner Evans.
                    (pause)
          Hey Jack. Sounds like you're starting
          to recover from last night.
                    (pause)
          No. I've been up for three hours, just
          sitting here with Colin.
                    (pause)
          About ten minutes, I guess. Why don't
          you come over? I'll have Charlie put
          on another pot . . . or maybe you'd prefer
          a little "hair of the dog"?

Getting Started

THE FORMAT BOX

To help you understand the function and visualize the placement of the elements of the screenplay format, examples are set apart from the text by enclosing them in stylized boxes.

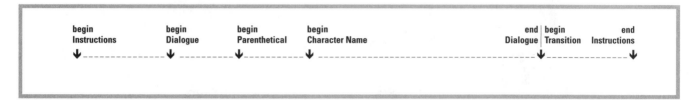

In the above box, consider the bordered area to represent *only* the typed portion of a screenplay page.

THE HEADER

On the first line of each page of the screenplay (except the first), a header is required.

Traditionally, a header includes these elements:

- The *page number*, which is aligned with the right margin. Each page (except the first) MUST be sequentially numbered.

- The *title* of the screenplay can appear on each page (except the first) on the same line as the page number but aligned with the left margin and underlined.

  Increasingly, the use of the title in a header is optional.

- Two *blank lines* MUST separate the header from the first lines of text.

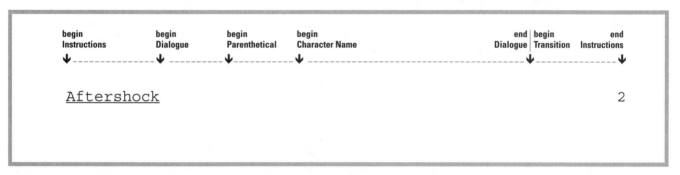

Aftershock, p. 2.

MARGIN SETTINGS

If you are using a standard word-processing program, you will have to set your own margins. The following guidelines will help.

NOTES:

- All margin settings are measured from the left edge of the page.

- Although the margin settings are approximate, you will want to keep them as close as possible to the specified dimensions.

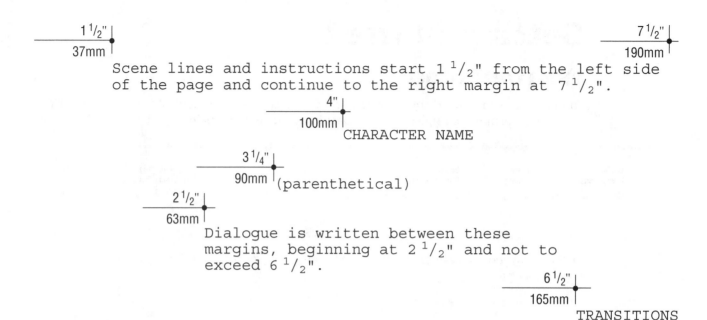

Scene lines and instructions start 1 $^1/_2$" from the left side of the page and continue to the right margin at 7 $^1/_2$".

CHARACTER NAME

(parenthetical)

Dialogue is written between these margins, beginning at 2 $^1/_2$" and not to exceed 6 $^1/_2$".

TRANSITIONS

The Elements of a Screenplay

HOW SCREENPLAYS BEGIN AND END

A few lines down from the top of the first page is the title of the screenplay. It is usually typed in ALL CAPS and centered. It also can be underlined.

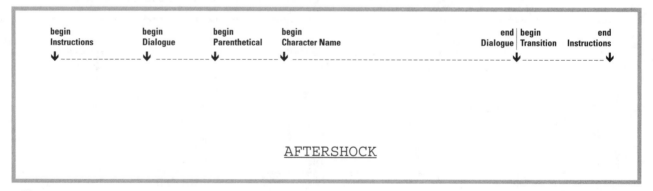

Aftershock, p. 1.

The text of every screenplay begins with blank lines (like a blank screen in a movie theater) and must FADE IN: to the first image. Therefore, the first words of the screenplay are

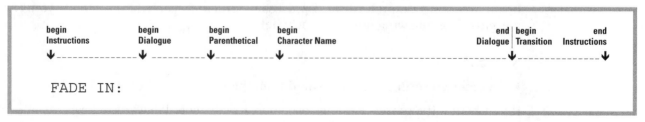

Aftershock, p. 1.

NOTE:

A colon ALWAYS follows the FADE IN:

Similarly, every screenplay ends with FADE OUT: and THE END.

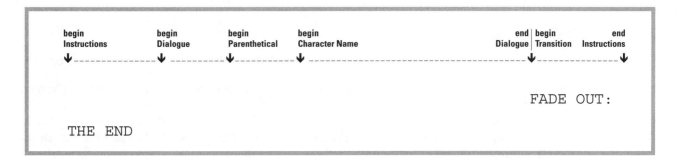

Between the FADE IN: and FADE OUT: the screenplay is composed of a series of scenes.

1. SCENE LINES

Each scene, regardless of whether it is a new location or a repeated location, is introduced with the scene line.

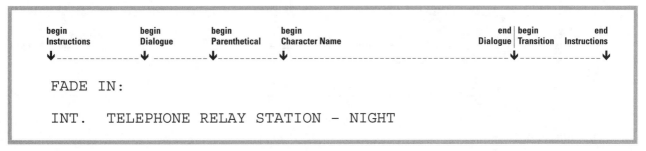

Aftershock, p. 1.

GENERAL RULES

The scene line

- is ALWAYS aligned between $1\frac{1}{2}$" and $7\frac{1}{2}$" from the left side of the page
- is ALWAYS separated from whatever is above or below it by a single blank line
- is ALWAYS typed in ALL CAPS
- should be contained on a single line

Each scene line has three components: the *staging*, the *location*, and the *time*.

THE STAGING

The first component in the scene line provides the most basic information about the set-up of the scene.

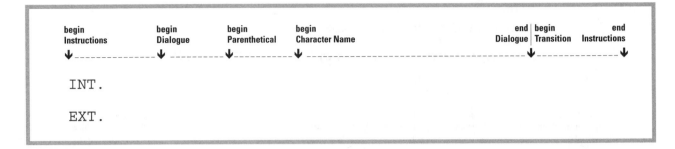

The staging is ALWAYS abbreviated and followed by a period. There are only two choices for a scene:

- INT. for an *interior* set, informing the reader that the scene takes place in an inside environment

- EXT. for an *exterior* set, specifying an outside environment

THE LOCATION

The second component in the scene line is the location in which the scene takes place.

- The location follows the INT. or EXT. designation and is separated from it by two character spaces.

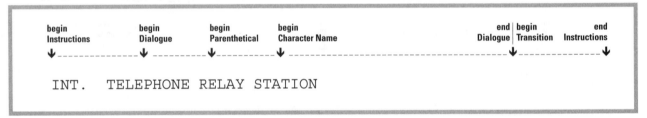

Aftershock, p. 1.

- *Do not abbreviate* any words in the location component of the scene line. For example, use

    INT.   APARTMENT

    rather than

    INT.   APT.

VERY IMPORTANT:

It is absolutely essential that every specific location be distinguished from every other location.

- If Joe lives in an apartment, then you can call that location

    INT.   APARTMENT

    But if, in the same screenplay, Bob also has an apartment in which scenes will take place, then you can no longer use INT.   APARTMENT as a location for Bob's apartment.

To eliminate any confusion, one solution is to call each apartment location by the resident's name:

```
INT.   BOB'S APARTMENT
```

```
INT.   JOE'S APARTMENT
```

- Once a specific location has been identified in the scene line, all subsequent scenes taking place in that location MUST be identified in *exactly* the same way.

Depending on the different locations within your screenplay, you must determine the best method to identify the locations to your reader. Whatever method you choose, the designations must be clear and concise.

FIRST NOTE:

The location identifies where the activity and dialogue take place. For example:

- If John lives in a one-room apartment (so that the entire area of the apartment is visible), then the location should be identified as

```
INT.   JOHN'S APARTMENT
```

However, if John lives in a multi-room apartment and John is currently in his bedroom (so that the other rooms are concealed from view), then the scene line must read

```
INT.   JOHN'S BEDROOM
```

or

```
INT.   JOHN'S APARTMENT, BEDROOM
```

- If the activity is going to occur in several rooms of John's apartment, you need to create separate scenes (and scene lines) for each appropriate room. You would specify

```
INT.   JOHN'S BEDROOM
```

If John then moves into the living room, the next location would be

```
INT.   JOHN'S LIVING ROOM
```

And if John then moves into the kitchen, that location would be

```
INT.   JOHN'S KITCHEN
```

- If you clearly establish that the rooms are in John's apartment, it may not be necessary to continually re-identify each room with John's name.

If the first scene is

```
INT.   JOHN'S BEDROOM
```

and then John moves into his kitchen, the next scene could be

```
INT.   KITCHEN
```

It would be assumed that it's John's kitchen.

You must be certain, however, that there is no confusion about whose kitchen it is. If there is any doubt, play it safe and define the location as

```
INT.   JOHN'S KITCHEN
```

SECOND NOTE:

Remember that once you identify a location in the scene line, the scene MUST take place in that location.

- Most locations are immediately clear, such as

  INT. JOHN'S BEDROOM

- But what if John walks from the bedroom to the little balcony just off the bedroom?

  If the activity on the balcony can be viewed from the bedroom, then you can keep what happens on the balcony under the same scene line.

  However, if it is more appropriate to re-locate the activity and dialogue to the balcony, then you must have a new scene with a new scene line, such as

  EXT. JOHN'S BALCONY

THIRD NOTE:

How detailed should the location be?

Because you need to keep the location concise, how you write the location will usually depend on two primary considerations.

- One consideration is how generally or specifically to define the location. If you write a location that is non-specific within a much larger or complex environment, such as

  INT. ALBUQUERQUE AIRPORT

  you are informing the reader that no specific area within the airport is important. The scene could occur anywhere inside the airport, and that decision is then left to the director.

  By specifically including ALBUQUERQUE in the location, you are informing the director that it is important that this particular airport be identified to the audience.

  If, however, the scene needs to take place in a specific area within the airport, then you need to create a location that includes that area. Such a location might be

  INT. ALBUQUERQUE AIRPORT, TICKETING AREA

- Another consideration is how much description to include in defining an environment. Whereas the previous situation examined a very large environment (the Albuquerque Airport) that could be limited (to the Ticketing Area), this situation concerns an already limited environment that could be further described.

  You could write any of the following:

  INT. CLASSROOM

  INT. COLLEGE CLASSROOM

  INT. COLLEGE BIOLOGY CLASSROOM

  In the first scene line, the location of CLASSROOM is left very general. It could be anything from a first-grade classroom to an adult education classroom.

  In the second and third scene lines, the location is more precise. It is not any classroom; it is specifically a COLLEGE CLASSROOM or even more specifically a COLLEGE BIOLOGY CLASSROOM.

FOURTH NOTE:

A scene line can take either of two common variations:

- Most often, the scene line will define a *specified location*, such as

  INT.   JOHN'S LIVING ROOM

  EXT.   PARKING LOT

  which limits the field of view to the area where the camera is placed.

- If the scene takes place in a more *generalized location*, you can write it as an open scene, such as

  EXT.   COLLEGE CAMPUS

  By identifying the scene in a generalized way, you are indicating that it is not important to your narrative to identify precisely where on the campus this scene takes place.

THE TIME

The third component of the scene line indicates the general time at which the scene begins.

- The time follows the location and is separated from it by a character space, then a dash, and then another character space.

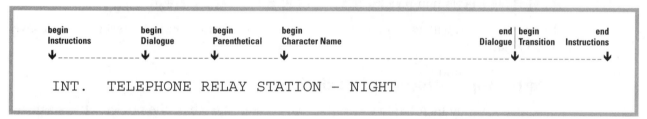

Aftershock, p. 1.

- The time component of the scene line is most typically specified as a simple

  DAY

  or

  NIGHT

- However, the time component *can* define a more precise period of the day or night. For example,

  DAWN

  MORNING

  AFTERNOON

  MID-AFTERNOON

  RUSH HOUR

  LATE EVENING

  In no case, however, can you be any more specific in the scene line than a visual approximation. You CANNOT specify an exact time, such as 3:30 P.M., in the scene line. If such a specific time is required, you need to do this in the instructions.

- When there is no lapse of time from one scene to the next, the time element in the scene line could simply be

CONTINUOUS

Or if the time lapse is very brief, then you could use something like

MOMENTS LATER

A FEW MINUTES LATER

AN EXCEPTION:

If a scene takes place in a location in which there is no way to gauge the visible time (DAY or NIGHT), then that element is omitted from the scene line, as in

INT.   ELEVATOR

INT.   MINE SHAFT

INT.   SUBMARINE

In these examples, it is assumed that there are no windows in the elevator and no openings in the mine shaft. Therefore, there would be no indication of a visual time reference (daylight or darkness).

ADDING SPECIFICS TO THE SCENE LINE

On occasion, you will want to add another piece of information to the scene line to save later explanation.

Identifying a Historical Period

If the narrative takes place in a specific year or era other than the present, the scene line allows you to include such a reference.

For example, a scene line could be written as

EXT.   PARIS, FRANCE - DAY (1946)

EXT.   CHICAGO, ILLINOIS - DAY (1920s)

EXT.   FLORENCE, ITALY - DAY (THE RENAISSANCE)

Indicating a Mobile Situation

If a scene opens with a moving vehicle within the location, then that can be indicated in the scene line. For example, from the scene line

INT.   JOHN'S CAR - DAY (MOVING)

we would immediately know that John's car is being driven.

In a Character's Mind

Similarly, if a scene takes place in the mind of a character, that can be indicated in the scene line. For example,

EXT.   A FOOTBALL FIELD - DAY (FLASHBACK)

INT.   JAKE'S TAVERN - NIGHT (A FANTASY)

NOTE:

It is assumed that once you have identified a scene as, for example, a flashback, we remain in that flashback (for the single scene or all subsequent scenes) until another scene line parenthesis is used to change the circumstances. For example,

        INT.   JENNIFER'S BEDROOM - DAY (RETURN TO PRESENT)

        EXT.   PARKING AREA - NIGHT (RETURN TO REALITY)

2. INSTRUCTIONS (also called *actions* or *directions*)

Instructions impart the necessary detail to the essentials of the scene, describing such features as the characters, sets, props, and any necessary action and sound cues.

- It is generally best to keep the level of detail focused on the actions and dialogue that comprise the narrative. That is where your attention and the reader's interest should be directed.

- By describing the particular props and décor in a scene and how each character dresses or grooms, you can suggest such character information as personality type, emotional condition, religious affiliation, economic level, artistic taste, and so forth.

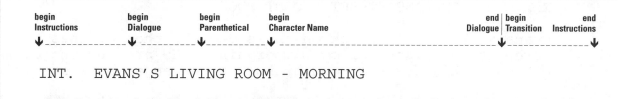

| begin Instructions | begin Dialogue | begin Parenthetical | begin Character Name | | end Dialogue | begin Transition | end Instructions |

```
INT.  EVANS'S LIVING ROOM - MORNING

The large impeccably neat room has high ceilings and tall
windows taking full advantage of the morning light.  One wall
has floor to ceiling book cases filled with leather-bound
volumes.  Another has a large marble fireplace.

In the center of the room facing the fireplace is a large
tufted leather sofa.  The coffee table is an old flat drawing
file with a glass top.  It contains a collection of Civil
War pistols.
```

Aftershock, p. 9. In this description, those items in Evans's living room that reveal aspects of his character are written into the instructions. These details suggest that Evans is wealthy, educated, and orderly; that he is a collector; and that he has good taste.

GENERAL RULES

Instructions:

- are ALWAYS aligned between 1 ¹/₂" and 7 ¹/₂" from the left side of the page

- are written in standard prose (sentences or fragments) with appropriate punctuation

- are written in block paragraphs separated by single blank lines.

Instructions generally cover information about the following:

- *Sets* which establish what décor and props are important to the scene

- *Characters* who are present, how they are dressed and what they are doing

- *Actions* which explain what happens as the characters interact with each other and their environment

- *Sounds* other than dialogue that may be needed

There is a general approach to writing instructions.

- First, *establish the scene*, describing only what is visually apparent in the location, and giving only as much detail as necessary.

  You cannot describe anything that cannot be seen, such as items in a desk drawer or behind a curtain, until they have been revealed.

  You do not need to itemize things that are generic and would ordinarily be present, such as furnishings, colors, arrangements, and so forth.

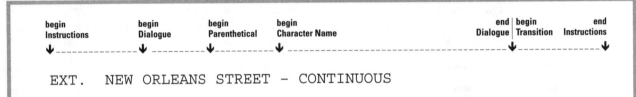

```
begin              begin         begin           begin                                      end | begin           end
Instructions       Dialogue      Parenthetical   Character Name                         Dialogue | Transition  Instructions
    ↓----------------↓----------↓-----------↓----------------------------------------------↓--------------↓

EXT.   NEW ORLEANS STREET - CONTINUOUS

Evans walks half a block on the sidewalk, then crosses the
street to a bright yellow Lamborghini.  He presses the alarm
button on his key ring and opens the passenger side door.
```

Aftershock, p. 2. In these instructions, the street environment is left vague because it is not important whether there are any activities or people on the street.

However, you MUST specify anything that is either unusual or essential to the scene.

```
begin              begin         begin           begin                                      end | begin           end
Instructions       Dialogue      Parenthetical   Character Name                         Dialogue | Transition  Instructions
    ↓----------------↓----------↓-----------↓----------------------------------------------↓--------------↓

INT.   EVANS'S LIVING ROOM - MORNING

The large impeccably neat room has high ceilings and tall
windows taking full advantage of the morning light.  One wall
has floor to ceiling book cases filled with leather-bound
volumes.  Another has a large marble fireplace.

In the center of the room facing the fireplace is a large
tufted leather sofa.  The coffee table is an old flat
drawing file with a glass top.  It contains a collection of
Civil War pistols.
```

Aftershock, p. 9. In this description, the library of leather-bound books and the collection of Civil War pistols are unusual items that provide clues to Evans's character.

- Next, *identify the characters* who are present at the time the scene opens and briefly explain what each is doing.

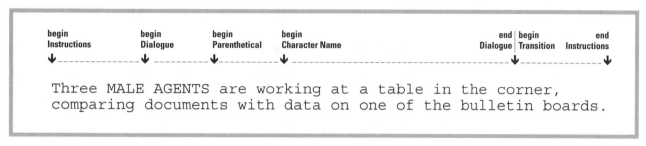

begin Instructions	begin Dialogue	begin Parenthetical	begin Character Name	end Dialogue	begin Transition	end Instructions

```
Three MALE AGENTS are working at a table in the corner,
comparing documents with data on one of the bulletin boards.
```

Aftershock, p. 6.

Identify any other characters at the time each enters the scene.

- Then proceed to *describe the activity* of the scene as it unfolds.

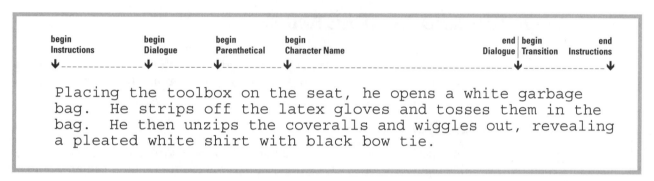

begin Instructions	begin Dialogue	begin Parenthetical	begin Character Name	end Dialogue	begin Transition	end Instructions

```
Placing the toolbox on the seat, he opens a white garbage
bag.  He strips off the latex gloves and tosses them in the
bag.  He then unzips the coveralls and wiggles out, revealing
a pleated white shirt with black bow tie.
```

Aftershock, p. 2.

VERY IMPORTANT:

In the instructions, you can ONLY reveal what can be seen and heard.

- You CANNOT tell what has happened or what will happen. You can only convey what is happening at the moment.

- You CANNOT provide any biographical, psychological, or situational information unless you can find a visual means to do so (such as a newspaper article, a television program, a computer screen, etc.).

How Much Detail to Provide

Another area in which judgment is required concerns the amount of detail you furnish about the location, about the situation, about the characters, and about what happens.

As the screenwriter, you want to create the feel of an environment. The production team will fill in the specifics.

- Providing too much detail defeats the blueprint nature of the format, and providing too little detail risks misinterpretation.

  Again, the rule of thumb is to offer the reader only enough detail to supply the basic ingredients of the scene. The reader's imagination will fill in the rest.

- Part of writing a good screenplay is to find that happy medium between the description being too fat or too lean.

As when reading a newspaper, it is easier to read and retain paragraph blocks of a few sentences than paragraph blocks of more formidable length. Paragraph blocks should be divided into logical parcels.

The Trick to Writing Instructions

Make the screenplay read like the film will be experienced. Because both the screenplay and the film are always taking place in the moment, you should always write in the **present tense.** It should be as though the screenplay is occurring as you are writing it and as the reader is reading it.

Although we have five physical senses, in the film medium you are strictly limited to only the senses of **sight** and **sound.** Attempts to appeal to balance (Imax, Omnivision), smell (Smell-O-Vision, Scratch and Sniff), and vibration (Sensurround) have been more experimental or faddish than mainstream.

INTRODUCING CHARACTERS

Each character must be *introduced* in the instructions the first time he or she physically appears in the screenplay. This includes not only major characters, but also supporting characters and even minor characters and groups that function as characters.

Naming Characters

When a character is introduced, his or her name (called the *character-name*) is ALWAYS typed in ALL CAPS regardless of whether the character is identified by a proper name, a profession, or an appearance. For example,

```
EVANS

AGENT ONE

DERELICT
```

Once a character has been introduced, all subsequent references to that character's name in the instructions should be written in a normal manner with initial caps.

```
Evans

Agent One

Derelict
```

Whichever character-name you choose to use, it is essential to use it consistently as the character-name.

- If you have introduced the character as WARNER EVANS in the instructions, then you will probably want to use the designation WARNER or EVANS for all future references.

  A caution: This means of identification is, of course, only helpful to the reader of the screenplay. In the viewing process, character-names need to be identified by some visual or oral means to the audience.

- Although the screenplay must consistently refer to each character by a specific character-name, different characters in dialogue may use other designations, such as nicknames, familiarities, titles, and so forth.

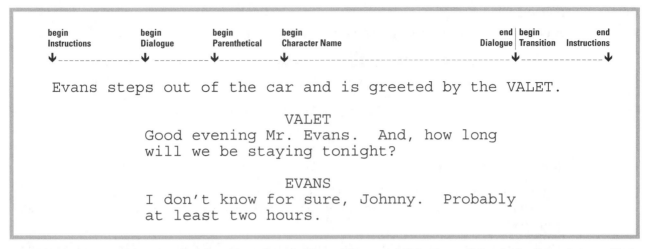

| begin Instructions | begin Dialogue | begin Parenthetical | begin Character Name | end Dialogue | begin Transition | end Instructions |

Evans steps out of the car and is greeted by the VALET.

                          VALET
          Good evening Mr. Evans. And, how long
          will we be staying tonight?

                          EVANS
          I don't know for sure, Johnny. Probably
          at least two hours.

Aftershock, p. 3. In this example, the valet refers to Warner Evans as "Mr. Evans." Similarly, the valet is called "Johnny" by Evans. Neither of these affects the character-name.

Describing Characters

As the screenwriter, you know who is a major character and who is a supporting or minor character because you have the entire story in mind. The reader, however, is in a different situation.

- A professional script reader, evaluating the merits of a screenplay, will immediately seek to identify the main characters and how they are going to interact. The amount of detail that you provide about a character's appearance and demeanor will give the reader a key to that character's importance in the script.

- As a guide, when characters are introduced, you need to make clear how important each is going to be by tailoring the description and context accordingly.

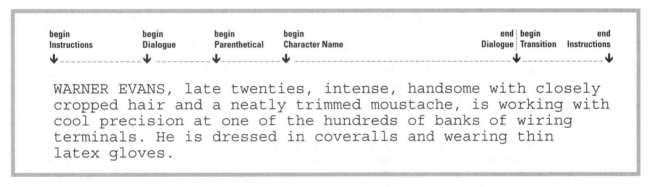

| begin Instructions | begin Dialogue | begin Parenthetical | begin Character Name | end Dialogue | begin Transition | end Instructions |

WARNER EVANS, late twenties, intense, handsome with closely
cropped hair and a neatly trimmed moustache, is working with
cool precision at one of the hundreds of banks of wiring
terminals. He is dressed in coveralls and wearing thin
latex gloves.

Aftershock, p. 1. The amount of description given to Warner Evans suggests that he will be a major character.

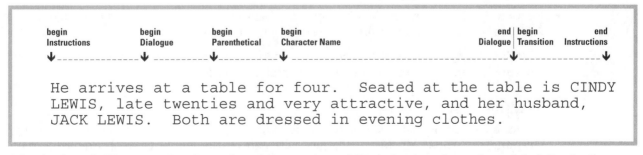

| begin Instructions | begin Dialogue | begin Parenthetical | begin Character Name | end Dialogue | begin Transition | end Instructions |

He arrives at a table for four. Seated at the table is CINDY
LEWIS, late twenties and very attractive, and her husband,
JACK LEWIS. Both are dressed in evening clothes.

Aftershock, p. 3. Because only a basic description is given of Cindy Lewis and even less of Jack Lewis, the reader will suspect that they are not as prominent to the narrative as, say, Warner Evans.

A VARIATION:

A character's age can also be assigned a numerical designation, such as

```
WARNER EVANS (late 20s), ruggedly handsome, dressed in . . .
```

or

```
Seated at the table is CINDY LEWIS, late 20s and very
attractive, . . .
```

What to Describe

What is important in describing a character are the objects and patterns that suggest an impression of the character's economic level, personal preferences, particular behaviors, and so on.

These factors are often related to external items: what kind of car the character drives, how the character decorates a personal space, what kind of order the residence or office has. These things and a multitude of others can reveal a great deal about a character.

What Not to Describe

Readers are not usually interested in such specifics as the color of a character's eyes, the texture of his or her skin, or his or her exact height or weight. It is best to keep such details more general, allowing for a wider range of casting.

Major Characters   (also called *leading* or *primary* characters)

Each major character needs to be personalized by a *character-name*.

- The character-names assigned to all major characters should be proper names. This is not necessary for lesser characters.

- What you name a character will often determine in part how the reader will respond to that character. For example, using the character-name WARNER is friendlier to the reader than EVANS, and both are more personal than WARNER EVANS.

When a major character is introduced, you also need to give a general description of him or her. Unless there is a narrative reason to do otherwise, you will want to provide a more complete profile of your major dominant characters than you will give to subordinate characters.

- Indicate the character's physical appearance, his or her sex (if it's not otherwise obvious), and an approximate age. The age must reflect the age that the character *appears* to be. If the character's actual age is significantly different from what is suggested by his or her appearance, then this must be revealed through dialogue or some other way.

- Generally describe what the character is wearing. Clothing often suggests something about the character's personality, profession, or situation.

- Finally, if they are relevant, include any significant details—distinguishing physical features, peculiar mannerisms, vocal patterns, and so on.

TWO WARNINGS:

- First, as tempting as it may be to create characters with distinctive attributes, keep in mind that those attributes will generate expectations about the character. For example, if you describe a character as having a prominent scar, you will create the expectation that the scar will in some way be significant to the narrative.

- Second, in describing a character, never make reference to particular actors or particular movies, such as

```
He walks with a John Wayne swagger.
```

and

```
Like the opening scenes of "Saving Private Ryan."
```

However, you could make reference to a public figure, such as

```
He speaks with the calculated precision of John F.
Kennedy.
```

Supporting Characters (also called *secondary* characters)

Although supporting characters often have very significant roles, they are less dominant than major characters. Descriptions are provided for supporting characters, but they tend to be less detailed than those provided for major characters.

- As is done with a major character, the first time a supporting character is mentioned, he or she should be identified in ALL CAPS.

- Like major characters, all supporting characters should be given proper names (such as Cindy and Jack).

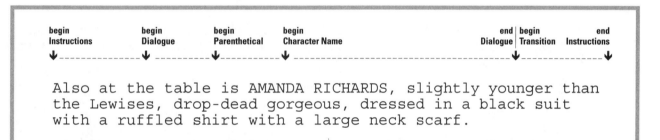

Aftershock, p. 4. In this example, Amanda Richards, is given a more detailed description than other characters, indicating that she will be a more important player—at least a supporting character and perhaps a major character.

Minor Characters (also called *bit* or *throwaway* characters)

Certainly, some of the characters in your screenplay will not be important enough to warrant individualized names and specific descriptions. These characters typically serve a *function* for a scene or two and then are discarded once their usefulness in the narrative has finished.

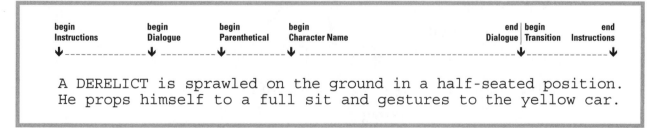

Aftershock, p. 2. Unlike the previous examples of Warner Evans, the Lewises, and Amanda Richards, for whom general descriptions were provided, there is no description for the Derelict. By omitting this description, you are informing the reader that it makes no difference what he looks like, what his age is, or how he is behaving; it only matters that he is a derelict.

- Even if a minor character is referred to by a proper name in dialogue, you may find it more useful to identify him or her by a profession, physique, gender, age, or the like—whatever best fixes that character's *function* in the script.

  For example, such labels as MEDICAL EXAMINER, FAT MAN, SEXY WOMAN, and OLD MAN indicate that the character is more important as a *type* than as an individual.

- If several minor characters are serving the same or similar functions, then they can be distinguished by assigning numbers or adjectives to the character-names, such as

  POLICEMAN 1 and POLICEMAN 2

  FIRST POLICEMAN and SECOND POLICEMAN

  TALL POLICEMAN and SLOPPY POLICEMAN

Groups (also called *extras*)

Similarly, groups can be reduced to certain types.

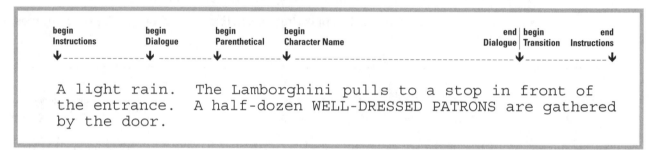

Aftershock, p. 3.

- A group can be identified by a one-word generality, such as

  CROWD

  STUDENTS

  WORKERS

  SOLDIERS

- You can be more descriptive by attaching an appropriate adjective, such as

  UNRULY CROWD

  COLLEGE STUDENTS

  FACTORY WORKERS

  UNIFORMED SOLDIERS

IDENTIFYING CHARACTER NAMES TO THE AUDIENCE

Remember that in the instructions, identifying a character by a personal name does not reveal the character's name to the audience.

Assuming that you have given your character a personal name, it is a good practice to identify him or her to the audience by that name as soon as possible.

- Most often, this is done verbally in dialogue when one character refers to another character by name.

- This also can be done visually by including a nameplate on a door, a signature on a paper, a name on a business card, and so on.

Either of these options must be done in a way that seems natural in the context of the narrative.

LIMITATIONS AND LIBERTIES ON INTRODUCING CHARACTERS

It is important to remember that you can ONLY describe what will be *seen* at the time the character is introduced.

- For example, suppose your character walks with a limp because he has an artificial leg, but the first time we see him, he is wearing long pants and is seated at a table in a restaurant. It would be inappropriate to mention the character's limp until he gets up to walk over to the cashier's station.

- Even then, all you would observe is that the character walks with a limp. To reveal that the limp is caused by the artificial leg, you must wait until someone mentions it in dialogue or we see the limb.

There Are Limitations to What You Can Reveal

In the instructions, you cannot provide information that is not visually apparent.

- You CANNOT reveal anything about the background, thoughts, or intentions of a character.

- You CANNOT reveal anything about where a character has come from or is going to.

- You CANNOT reveal anything about the way a character speaks until that character is actually heard.

But There Are Liberties That Can Stretch the Limitations

- As a rule, when describing the appearance of a character in the instructions, you CANNOT specify his or her nationality, background, personality, or feelings.

  For example, you could NOT write

  `He is Argentinean.`

  But you could write

  `He has Latin features.`

  You could NOT write

  `He has spent his life as a rough street cop.`

  But you could write

  `He looks as though he has been hardened by street life.`

- When introducing a character, you may find it helpful to provide the reader with behavioral qualities that assist in visualizing the situation.

  For example, you could write

  ```
  PHIL is not quite what Matt calls a friend but someone he
  tolerates in small doses.
  ```

  Or you could write

  ```
  MARLENE has all the right clothes, the right smile, the
  right words, the right touch.  But there's something about
  her that tries too hard.
  ```

- You can sometimes stretch the see-and-hear principle a bit if it assists the scene and if it is "actable."

  For example, you could include comments such as these in the instructions:

  ```
  Susan quickly seals the package.  She's nervous and trying
  too hard to appear natural.
  ```

  ```
  He nods as if to say that everything is under control.
  ```

  ```
  He sits behind the stick in the cockpit like he was born
  to fly.
  ```

  ```
  Nicole searches the man's face for some kind of reaction.
  ```

  ```
  Helen is a woman in her early thirties who would be much
  prettier if she didn't look so severe in both her choice
  of clothing and manner.
  ```

  These are all actable descriptions and therefore acceptable to include as written instructions. However, be guarded against over-extending such liberties.

WORDS THAT GET CAPPED

In addition to using CAPS to introduce characters in the instructions, there are established conventions for other elements that need to be typed in CAPS but only if they affect the narrative.

Those elements include:

- all essential costumes, props, and décor
- any important action, effect, or emphasis
- any required music or sounds

Although some of the following instances will require CAPPING, many will be judgment decisions.

Important Costumes, Props, and Décor

The instructions of a screenplay also serve to identify objects that are *essential* to the story or a particular character. For example,

- *Costumes*, which describe the clothing and accessories that the characters wear

- *Props*, which consist of the objects that are handled by the actors
- *Décor*, which is anything that is not handled by the actors (This is often called *dressing the set* and includes wall decorations and room furniture.)

All costumes, props, and décor that are *essential* to the narrative are to be written in ALL CAPS.

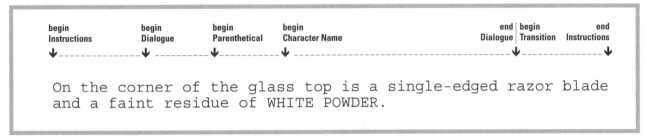

Aftershock, p. 9. In this example, the WHITE POWDER is identified with caps because it is specific and essential to the character. It will have a significant influence later in the narrative.

FIRST NOTE:

You CANNOT identify *every* costume, prop, or décor on the set. Ordinary objects that have no special significance to the narrative should be left to specialized members on the production team.

SECOND NOTE:

As a screenwriter, you often have to think about scenes ahead of the one you are writing.

- For example, if a certain prop is important to the story, you should CAP it when it first appears, regardless of whether it is important to that particular scene.
- Although the importance of a specific item or object may not be apparent at the time it appears, CAPPING it alerts the reader to its future importance.

An Important Action, Effect, or Emphasis

Occasionally, you will need to draw the reader's attention to an action, effect, or emphasis that is important to the dramatic effectiveness of the scene. You do this by CAPPING.

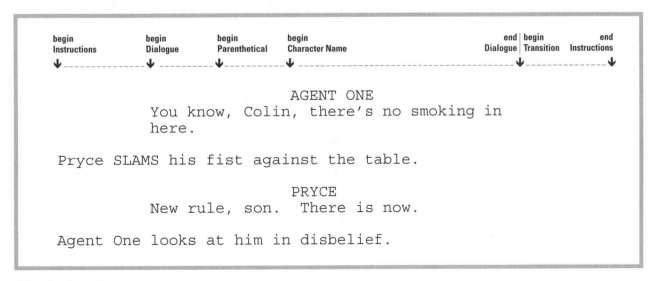

Aftershock, p. 8.

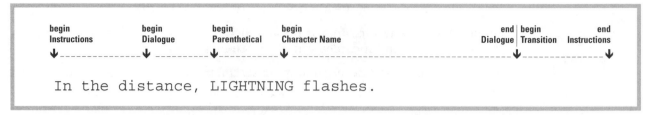

Aftershock, p. 3.

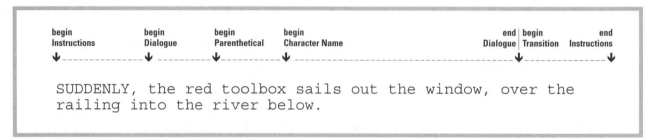

Aftershock, p. 2.

Indicating Music

Music can be essential to reveal important aspects of character, story, or place.

- If you need to call for music, it is best to be generic. For example,

    COUNTRY-WESTERN

    ROCK AND ROLL

    CLASSICAL

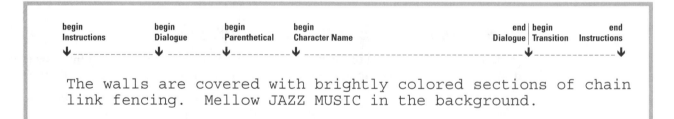

Aftershock, p. 3.

- If, however, a specific piece is required for the narrative, then identify it by title. For example,

    "THE ORANGE BLOSSOM SPECIAL"

    "JUMPIN' JACK FLASH"

    BEETHOVEN'S NINTH SYMPHONY

Unless music is essential to the scene, it is best to leave that decision to the director and composer.

IMPORTANT:

Background or thematic music is NEVER within the domain of the writer.

Certain Sounds

Just like you do not need to describe every detail of the set, you do not need to refer to every sound. But you do need to specify those sounds that affect the narrative.

For example, if a character is to answer a phone, you need to first state that the phone RINGS; if STREET NOISES are significant to the scene, then you need to cite them.

Aftershock, p. 9. Because we are inside the house with Evans, we cannot see the person at the door who is knocking. Therefore, the sound of the KNOCK must be capped.

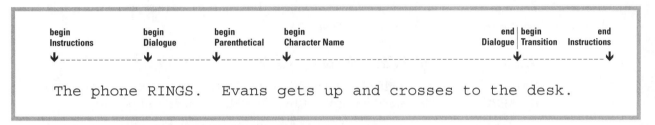

Aftershock, p. 10. Since we cannot see the ring of the phone, the sound of the RING must be capped.

How to Identify Sounds

It is usually the writer's choice whether to cap the word or phrase that best represents a sound.

If you write in the instructions that two gunshots are heard by the audience, you could write

    The SOUND of two gunshots shatters the silence.

- However, it would be more graphic to emphasize what the sound is

    Two GUNSHOTS shatter the silence.

- If the most important detail is that two gunshots are heard, then

    TWO GUNSHOTS shatter the silence.

- If what is most important is the effect of the gunshots, rather than the gunshots themselves, then

    Two gunshots SHATTER the silence.

With sounds, you generally want to CAP one of the following:

- What most accurately represents the *source* of the sound

- The *effect* that the sound has on the scene

Sounds That Do Not Get Capped

- In many situations, a sound may be written into the instructions but not affect the scene. Such a sound does NOT get capped. For example, a television may be playing in the background but the program has no significant bearing on the scene.

- As a rule, sounds that are *visibly clear* are NOT capped.

   For example, if a character in the scene walks to a door and we see him knock, the sound of the knock would NOT be capped.

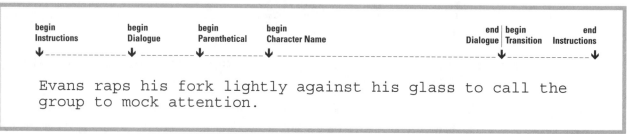

```
Evans raps his fork lightly against his glass to call the
group to mock attention.
```

Aftershock, p. 4. Because we see Evans rap the glass with his fork, that sound—although important—is not capped. However, if someone whom we do not see (for example, at an adjoining table) rapped a glass with a fork and it was important to the narrative that the people at this table heard that sound, then that rap would be capped (because we did not *see* the sound being made).

When to CAP and When Not to CAP

- CAPPED words can be effective only if they are used sparingly and appropriately. If CAPPED words are used too frequently, their significance will be lost.

- The best way to know if CAPPED words are being overused is quite simply to see how they look on the page. If the page *looks* cluttered with CAPPED words, you need to re-think and re-write.

USING A NOTE

As much as the screenplay should read like the film will be viewed, providing certain explanations can save time and words and thus effectively assist the reader.

These explanations need to be set apart.

Such explanations can be conveyed to the reader through the use of a NOTE: in the instructions. NOTE: means "a note to the reader" that provides basic information about the look or sound of the story and that will be helpful in imagining the screenplay as a film.

- In a screenplay, it is assumed that the story takes place in reality, in present time, and in color unless you indicate otherwise.

   The NOTE: device can be used to explain something unusual to the reader.

```
NOTE:  This space is actually a makeshift office in a
warehouse, the kind of unit that can be loaded into a tractor
trailer and relocated at a moment's notice.
```

Aftershock, p. 6.

- The NOTE: can also be helpful when a repetitive action would become annoying if cited every time it occurs.

  For example, if the screenplay is set on a military base, where required salutes are standard and numerous, you could use a NOTE: to explain that all salutes are given and returned in the appropriate manner. This, then, would relieve you of having to write such an instruction every time it occurs.

CAUTION:

You should never use a NOTE: unless it is absolutely necessary. The narrative should sufficiently explain itself.

REFINING THE WRITING OF INSTRUCTIONS

Having a good story and interesting characters is crucial to any screenplay. What supports the narrative is the wording you choose to convey it. A few suggestions may assist you in writing instructions.

Find an Effective Writing Style

A screenplay should be a "good read" without being literary.

- Although using all simple sentences certainly and directly gets to the details, it can make the screenplay dull to read. For example,

```
The mechanic steps out from behind the car.  He is
thirtyish and wears glasses.  He has long black hair.
His face is wrinkled.  He is wearing a blue uniform.
```

- At the other extreme, literary writing—flowery and complex—can easily read as pretentious. For example,

```
The mechanic ambulates from behind the vehicle.  Wearing
dark-rimmed spectacles and sporting a cascading black
mane, his thinly-featured visage is embroidered with
embedded furrows that connote existential tribulation.
The man displays his blue uniform as if the petroleum that
stains the fabric was a medal of honor.
```

- The object is to develop a style that is clear and spiced with some color. For example,

```
The car slaloms around the rush-hour traffic.

It is a beautiful autumn day.  The sun glistens through
the mist as it slowly rises above the water's glassy
surface.

Dennis bends down over his mother and plants a sticky
chocolate kiss on her cheek.
```

The descriptive passages need to be written in a style somewhere between Dick-and-Jane and Henry James.

Use the Simple Present Verb Form

The same activity can be expressed as

```
The bus pulls up to a street corner.
```

or

```
The bus is pulling up to a street corner.
```

The first expression (*pulls*) is grammatically the simple present form of the verb, while the second (*is pulling*) the present progressive verb tense,

In screenwriting, it is much more dynamic and direct to use simple present.

A COMMON EXCEPTION:

When a scene begins and activity is *already occurring*, it is appropriate (even preferable) to use the present progressive form. However, you should shift into the simple present when describing new activity. For example,

```
EXT.   URBAN STREET - DAY

The bus is pulling up to a street corner.  It stops and
Angelina gets on.
```

Consider *What Is* Rather Than *What Isn't*

Avoid using negatives, such as

```
She is neither homely nor attractive.
```

Rather than stating *what isn't*, it's more descriptive to state *what is*, such as

```
She is plain.
```

Using Abbreviations and Acronyms

- It is preferable not to use abbreviations and other shortcuts. For example, use

  ```
  background   instead of   b.g.
  ```

  Some abbreviations, however, have become preferable to the complete wording, especially when applied to titles and ranks. For example,

  ```
  Ph.D.   instead of   Doctor of Philosophy

  Sgt.   instead of   Sergeant
  ```

- Common acronyms are much like legitimate words and should be considered as such. For example,

  ```
  DNA   instead of   deoxyribonucleic acid
  ```

- It is preferable to use numbers where it would be unwieldy to write them out. For example,

  ```
  1992   instead of   Nineteen ninety-two
  ```

  ```
  $1,512,753.96   instead of   One million five hundred twelve
  thousand seven hundred fifty-three dollars and ninety-six
  cents.
  ```

Avoid *We see* and *We hear*

Remember, what you describe is what the reader will see and hear.

* It is amateurish to begin a descriptive comment with something that is clearly unnecessary. For example,

```
We see John light his cigarette.
```

or

```
John is seen as he lights his cigarette.
```

should be written simply as

```
John lights his cigarette.
```

Similarly,

```
We hear the sound of the hammer as it hits the nail.
```

or

```
The sound of the hammer as it hits the nail is heard.
```

should be more simply written as

```
The hammer strikes the nail.
```

Because what you describe is what the reader will see and hear, it is superfluous—even annoying—to remind him or her of the obvious.

* This also applies to characters who are about to speak:

```
John says . . .
John is talking . . .
```

which is immediately followed by John's dialogue.

The dialogue-block indicates not only what is spoken but also the character who speaks it. Again, it is a waste of words to state the obvious.

Therefore, strive to avoid such unnecessary expressions as "We see, . . ." "We hear, . . ." "He says, . . ." "He is talking, . . ." and the like.

Word Choice Is Important

You need to give the reader a specific image in words of what is to appear on the screen. Consequently, the words you select, especially verbs, are very important in creating that impression.

```
The men meander across the bridge.
The men race across the bridge.
The men march across the bridge.
```

For each description, the image created is different. Each depends on the choice of words used to describe how the men moved across the bridge.

Avoid Overly Technical Jargon and Detail

It is frequently tempting to show off expertise in a certain field by spicing a screenplay with descriptions that, although technically accurate, are obscure to most readers. For example,

```
Tony pushes the starboard control lever into forward and
the port into reverse.  He spins the skiff and skillfully
backs the vessel into a narrow slip.  An attendant jumps
to the gunnel with some docking lines.  He steps down to
the cockpit and brings two lines through the transom and
secures them to the stern cleats.
```

It is unlikely that such terminology and detail will be familiar to most readers. By including it, you risk losing the reader because it will be too difficult to follow the action you are describing. The previous passage, for example, might be written more simply as

```
Tony backs the boat into his docking spot.  An attendant
hops aboard and secures it with the ropes.
```

NOTE:

Although this applies to writing description, it does not apply to writing dialogue. If a character uses such jargon because of his profession or personality, then you need to write it that way.

Check the Order in Which Detail Is Presented

This is an important aspect of screenwriting that can create a problem for the reader. Consider the following example:

```
EXT.  MANSION, ENTRANCE DOOR - DAY

John arrives and rings the bell.  The Butler, dressed in a
black tuxedo, walks through the foyer of the mansion.  He
opens the door and escorts John inside.
```

Since the scene takes place outside (EXT.) the mansion, we wouldn't be able to see the Butler on the inside until he opens the door. A simple rewording would eliminate the problem:

```
EXT.  MANSION, ENTRANCE DOOR - DAY

John arrives and rings the bell.  The door opens and the
Butler, dressed in a black tuxedo, appears and escorts
John inside.
```

Don't Add Unnecessary Details and Traits

Visual details of the setting and décor and character traits of appearance and mannerisms can be very helpful in establishing situations and personalities. However, including details and traits simply for the sake of including details and traits can be misleading to the reader.

- As an example, you might write a character description such as

```
In his early twenties, SEYMOUR proudly displays his
weightlifter's physique, blemished only by a prominent
scar above his knee.
```

It is unlikely that the reader will forget the scar, and it is likely that the reader will expect the scar to have something to do with Seymour's character or the story's development.

If the word `scar` were in caps, it would signal the reader that the scar will serve some *significant* narrative purpose; if it doesn't, you risk either confusing or frustrating the reader.

- Or you might write a description such as

```
On his desk is a lamp with an elaborate duck decoy beside
it.
```

If the duck decoy is intended to reveal that the character has a penchant or fetish for ducks or that he has a fondness for these kinds of tokens, then you are suggesting that something will be made of this later.

Details like the scar and the duck decoy are commonly called *set-ups*. A set up is something that seems to have little meaning at the time but will have a *pay-off* at some future moment in the narrative.

Preserve the Emphasis of Importance

```
On top of the cabinet is a framed photograph of Rebecca in
an affectionate embrace with a man.
```

In this passage, the photograph serves to indicate that Rebecca has or had a relationship with a man, and no special importance is attributed to the photograph or the man.

```
On top of the cabinet is a framed PHOTOGRAPH of Rebecca in
an affectionate embrace with a man.
```

```
On top of the cabinet is a framed photograph of Rebecca in
an affectionate embrace with a MAN.
```

In these two examples, the emphasis has been changed. The first example indicates that the viewer's attention should be on the PHOTOGRAPH because it is capped. No special importance is attached to the specific man in the photograph.

In the second example, however, the emphasis has shifted to the romantic nature of the image. Because MAN is capped, we would expect that he will be given special importance in the story.

3. THE DIALOGUE-BLOCK

The dialogue element, called the *dialogue-block*, of the screenplay format consists of three components:

- the *character-name* specifies which character is speaking the dialogue

- the *dialogue* reveals what is said by that character

- a *parenthetical*, when necessary, instructs how or to whom the character speaks the dialogue

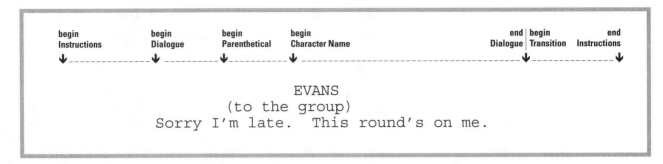

GENERAL RULES

The dialogue-block

- ALWAYS contains the character-name and dialogue, and it MAY, if helpful, also contain parenthetical instruction

- is ALWAYS single spaced with no blank lines that internally separate the individual components

- is ALWAYS preceded and followed by a single blank line

CHARACTER-NAMES

A character-name is the designation used for the speaker of the dialogue that follows.

Character-names

- are ALWAYS written in CAPS on the first line of the dialogue-block

- are ALWAYS indented 4" from the left side of the page

Also, once a character-name has been established, you MUST consistently use *that* name for *that* character.

For example, if you've introduced the character as COLIN PRYCE in the instructions, then you will probably want to use the designation COLIN or PRYCE in the dialogue-block.

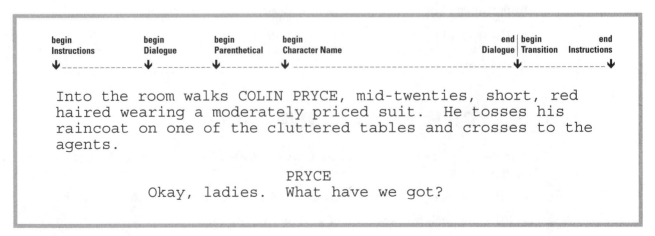

In the above example, COLIN PRYCE is introduced because it is the first time he appears in the screenplay. Therefore, his name is capped and the detail of his description indicates that he is an important character.

His character-name in the dialogue-block is PRYCE, and for all subsequent dialogue, his character-name will be PRYCE.

DIALOGUE

Everything that the actor speaks and that is heard by the audience is dialogue.

Dialogue

- is ALWAYS indented between $2\frac{1}{2}$" and $6\frac{1}{2}$" from the left side of the page
- is ALWAYS written in basic prose with initial caps and proper punctuation

Emphasis in Dialogue

As in proper prose, all appropriate punctuation must be observed.

- Quotation marks (single or double) may be used if the character is deliberately intending to emphasize a particular word or phrase. For example, a character might say

      What do you mean when you say "He
      got away with it"?

  But if a character is reciting a passage from a book or singing the lyrics to a song, quotation marks are generally not used.

- To emphasize a particular word or phrase, you should <u>underline</u> it. For example,

      He did <u>what</u>?

VERY IMPORTANT:

Do *not* use CAPS or *italics* or **bold** for emphasis. CAPS have special applications for emphasis in the instructions; italics and bold are not used in any element of the screenwriting format.

Hyphenating Dialogue

When writing dialogue, never break words with hyphens to accommodate the right margin. Dialogue is easier to read when words are kept whole, rather than hyphenated.

Off-Screen and Voice-Over Cues

Usually, a character who is speaking dialogue is visually present within the scene. However, there are two important exceptions: off-screen and voice-over.

The *off-screen* (O.S.) and *voice-over* (V.O.) cues

- ALWAYS follow the character-name on the same line
- are ALWAYS enclosed in parentheses
- are ALWAYS abbreviated in upper case

Off-Screen (O.S.)

Any character who is part of the scene but not visible to the audience at the time of speaking is considered to be off-screen.

- The most frequent use of (O.S.) is when a character who is not physically present in the scene speaks dialogue from a nearby location—a location close enough that, if called on to do so, the character could enter the scene.

  Such a character might be speaking from a room outside the view of the scene or from behind a concealed area of the scene.

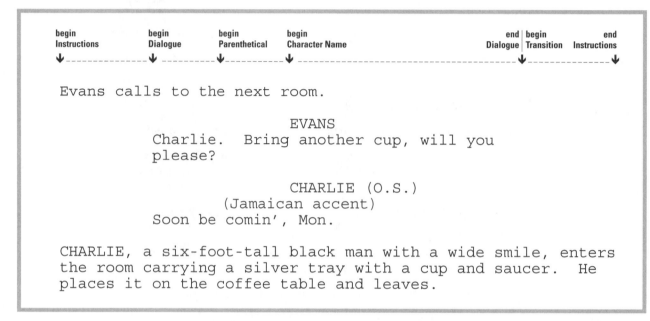

Aftershock, p. 9. In this example, Evans and Pryce are in the living room. Charlie, however, is in another room. Because Charlie is not in view but his voice is heard, his dialogue is off-screen (O.S.).

- If the (O.S.) is spoken by a character who has already been introduced or if it is obvious by the context who is speaking, then use the assigned character-name:

  CHARLIE (O.S.)

  If, however, the character has not yet been introduced or his or her identify must remain concealed, then the voice could be designated as

  VOICE (O.S.)

  MALE VOICE (O.S.)

  CHILD'S VOICE (O.S.)

Voice Over (V.O.)

There are three applications of the voice-over device:

1. *A voice heard through a mechanical device.* The (V.O.) convention is most commonly used when an unseen character's voice is heard through a mechanical device, such as a telephone, a radio, an intercom, a tape recording, an answering machine, or a public address system.

```
Pryce returns to the table where he tossed his coat.  He
clears a small work area.  He picks up the phone and dials.

                    VOICE (V.O.)
                (over phone)
            Dallas Center.

                    PRYCE
                (into phone)
            Agent Phillip Barnes, please.

                    VOICE (V.O.)
                (over phone)
            One moment please.

Pryce sorts through one of the piles of papers in front of
him.
```

Aftershock, p. 7. In this example, we see and hear Pryce as he speaks into the phone. However, we do not see the person on the other end; we only hear his or her voice through the phone, indicated by the use of (V.O.).

A VARIATION:

Instead of (over phone), the term (filtered) could be used:

```
                    VOICE (V.O.)
                (filtered)
            Dallas Center

                    PRYCE
                (into phone)
            Agent Phillip Barnes, please.

                    VOICE (V.O.)
                (filtered)
            One moment please.
```

2. ***The voice of a narrator.*** The (V.O.) convention is required when the dialogue is spoken by an *unseen* narrator.

   If the narrator is also a character who appears in the screenplay, then the character-name would be the same as the character-name in the story, For example,

   ```
                    JOHN (V.O.)
   ```

   However, if the narrator is an unidentified voice—not a character—then you would simply use

   ```
                    NARRATOR (V.O.)
   ```

3. ***The thoughts of a character.*** The (V.O.) device also applies when a character is visually present and what is heard are the thoughts of that character.

Continued Dialogue (cont'd)

Another instance in which a parenthesis accompanies a character-name occurs when a character's dialogue continues after being broken by an instruction.

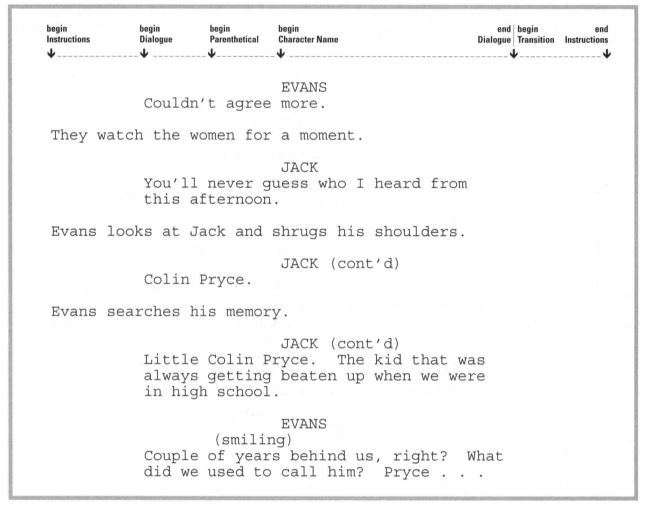

Aftershock, p. 5.

The (cont'd) convention

- ALWAYS follows the character-name on the same line
- is ALWAYS enclosed in parentheses
- is ALWAYS abbreviated in lower case

Advanced Dialogue Techniques

There are two fundamental directives about writing dialogue:

- The dialogue you write for your characters must be true to the way real flesh-and-blood people speak.
- At the same time, your characters must speak as individuals, not simply as projections of the way the writer would speak.

The Way People Talk

You must not only endow your characters with certain physical distinctions but also with certain vocal distinctions. The characters who populate your story can't all speak the same way. How they speak and relate to others must be consistent with their individual personalities.

You must consider such variables as

- *physical limitations*, such as speech impairments and native accents
- *educational level*, which affects the choice and complexity of a character's words and thoughts
- *regional or environmental background*, which frequently incorporates the use of slang and idiom
- *age level*, for example, a 12-year-old will not speak the same way as an octogenarian
- *professional level*, for example, an astrophysicist will not likely speak the same way as a stevedore

You must also consider the more subtle factors of motivations, expectations, goals, self-concepts, and the like that each character possesses.

Slang and Idiom

Slang and idioms must reflect characters' normal use of language. At the same time, you must be careful to consider your audience.

- If the slang or idiom is in common usage, there will be no problem with the audience understanding its meaning.

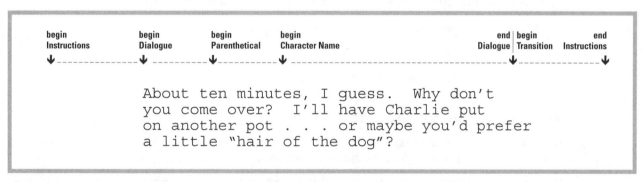

Aftershock, p. 10. The idiom "hair of the dog" refers to having another drink to ease the hangover from the previous night. This is a common idiom that is easily understood and requires no explanation.

- However, if the slang or idiom is limited to a select group, geographical location, or time period, then you must either trust the audience to pick up the meaning from the context or you must find a way to translate it for them.

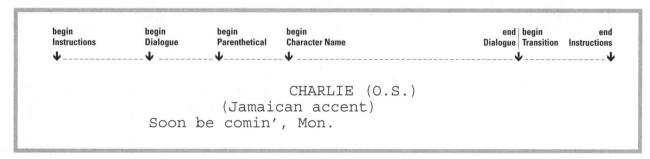

Aftershock, p. 9. "Soon be comin'" is a Jamaican expression that, although not used by Americans, can be understood by context.

Accents

If a character speaks with a distinctive regional dialect or foreign accent, you should indicate this by noting it either as a parenthetical or in the instruction.

- You should not attempt to simulate phonetic spellings for quirky dialogue. For example, if one of your characters comes from the deep South, it's better not to write "yawl" for "you all," even though the former is the way it would be spoken. Let the actor contribute the interpretation.

- If, however, a character comes from a foreign country and speaks in broken English, you could write it as such. For example,

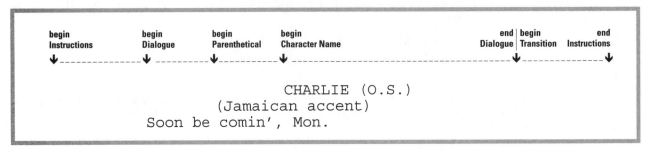

Aftershock, p. 9.

NOTE:

If Charlie were a more important character with substantial dialogue, it would be more emphatic to state his Jamaican accent in the instructions. For example,

```
Charlie speaks with a Jamaican accent.

                    CHARLIE (O.S.)
          Soon be comin', Mon.
```

Technical Language and Jargon

If the use of technical language is important to establishing the professional credibility of a character, then that character must speak as a professional.

For example, surgeons use names of drugs and instruments, astronauts use aerospace terminology, and police officers use numerical code designations. Such usage is perfectly appropriate to each character's dialogue, even if the exact meanings of the particular terms are unfamiliar.

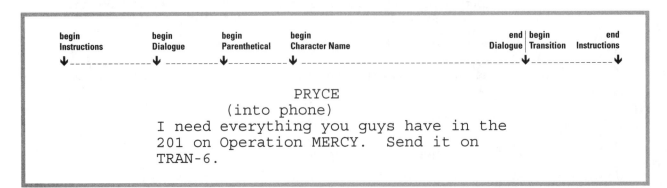

Aftershock, p. 7. In this example, it's not important that we know what a "201" is or what "Operation MERCY" or "TRAN-6" means. It's only important that the dialogue sounds like professionals speaking to each other.

Incomplete Sentences

Sometimes, staccato-like wording can add color and effect. For example,

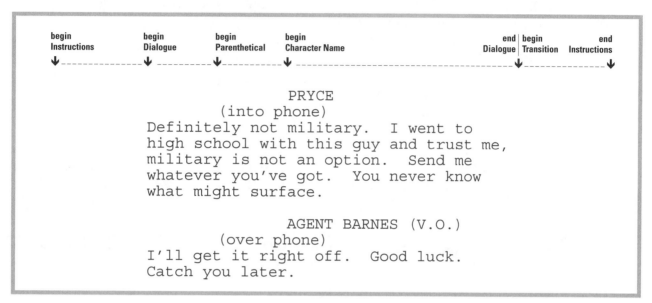

Aftershock, p. 8.

Ellipses

An ellipsis (. . .) is a useful mechanism for simulating speech, usually indicating either the way a sentence should be spoken or that a sentence will not be completed.

Depending on context, an ellipsis can mean that

- the character is interrupted before a sentence can be finished

- the character simply doesn't finish a thought and it trails off

- the character pauses in the middle of a sentence, as though hesitating, thinking, or changing the thought or perhaps for dramatic effect

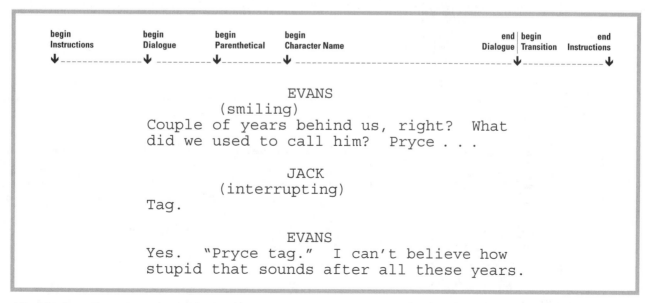

Aftershock, p. 5. In this example, the ellipsis indicates that Evans does not complete the sentence because he is interrupted by Jack.

- When such a situation occurs, a parenthetical `(interrupting)` must be added to specify the character who does the interrupting.

- Clearly, if the parenthetical `(interrupting)` was omitted, then the exchange would have a different interpretation:

> EVANS
>   (smiling)
> Couple of years behind us, right? What
> did we call him? Pryce . . .
>
>   JACK
>   Tag.

This use of an ellipsis would indicate that Evans simply trails off because he doesn't recall the nickname. Jack is not interrupting Evans but just supplying the reference.

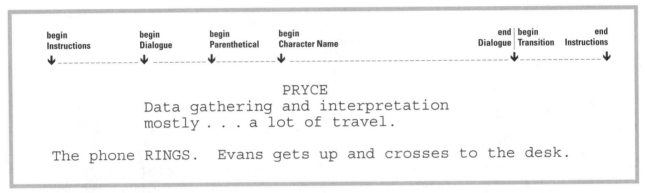

Aftershock, p. 10. In this example, Pryce tries to avoid giving a direct answer to the question about his profession by hesitating in mid-sentence. The ellipsis indicates his hesitation before finishing the thought.

Indistinct Voices and Non-Scripted Dialogue

These forms of talk typically do not need to be written into the script:

- If the actual dialogue is so inconsequential (it is usually reserved for background), it would be needlessly distracting to write it.

  On the production set, the director will typically instruct the background people to converse or react among themselves.

- If, for instance, it is important to a scene to have characters engaged in idle conversation and it makes no difference specifically what their dialogue contains, you could simply use a term like CHATTER in the instructions.

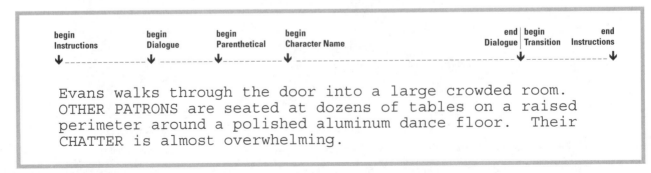

Aftershock, p. 3.

- In a similar instance, you might want characters talking to each other while also indicating that their specific exchange or exchanges are superficial. You could use the term AD LIB or AD LIBBING.

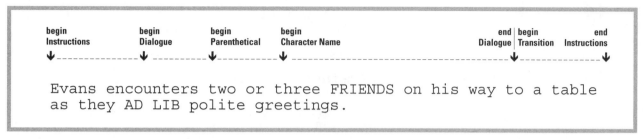

```
Evans encounters two or three FRIENDS on his way to a table
as they AD LIB polite greetings.
```

Aftershock, p. 3. In this case, you are indicating the superficial nature of the greetings without writing any specific dialogue. It would be unnecessary (even distracting) to write each exchange when it's so trivial and inconsequential to the narrative.

Additional Notes on Dialogue

Dialogue is perhaps the most difficult aspect of screenwriting to master, for several reasons:

- It must simulate actual conversation so that the reader will accept it as natural.
- It must compress and streamline so the reader won't get bored or impatient.
- The characters must speak as individuals, not simply as projections of how the writer would speak.
- As in real-life conversation, the characters can use slang, idiom, repetition, contractions, profanities, broken sentences, and incomplete thoughts.

The power of screenplay dialogue cannot be overestimated. A single line of dialogue may seem ordinary on the page, but on screen, it can have enduring cultural significance.

```
Here's looking at you, kid.

Go ahead.  Make my day.

I'll be back.
```

Screenplay dialogue is most often at its best when it is short and crisp.

Integrating Dialogue and Instructions

It is common practice to combine instructions concerning the activity of the scene with the dialogue that passes between the characters. This is especially useful when activities and vocals are naturally coordinated.

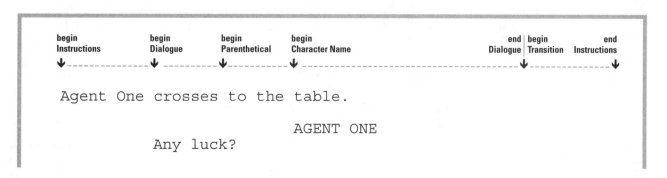

```
Agent One crosses to the table.

                        AGENT ONE
            Any luck?
```

```
                         PRYCE
                      (irritated)
            Dallas says he's clean as a whistle.

                       AGENT ONE
            You know, Colin, there's no smoking in
            here.

   Pryce SLAMS his fist against the table.

                         PRYCE
            New rule, son.  There is now.

   Agent One looks at him in disbelief.
```

Aftershock, p. 8.

PARENTHETICALS

Parentheticals are a convenient device to convey specific information about how the dialogue is to be said.

Parentheticals

* are ALWAYS placed on separate lines

* are ALWAYS indented $3\frac{1}{4}$" from the left side of the page

* are ALWAYS enclosed by parentheses

* are restricted to words, phrases, and fragments

* ALWAYS apply to the dialogue that immediately follows it

```
begin          begin         begin         begin                                    end│begin            end
Instructions   Dialogue      Parenthetical Character Name                       Dialogue│Transition  Instructions
↓------------- ↓-----------  ↓----------   ↓-------------------------------------------↓--------------↓

                         EVANS
            That.
                      (pointing to the front of
                      his shirt)
            And these damned studs.  You'd think
            someone would invent a shirt stud that
            didn't require four hands to install.

   They all laugh.  Amanda reaches over and checks the row of
   studs on Evans's shirt.  She adjusts his bow tie and gives
   him a kiss.

                         CINDY
                      (to Amanda and Evans)
            Well.  You got us here.  And all
            dressed up I might add.  What gives?
```

Aftershock, p. 4.

Parentheticals need to be concise and direct, indicating such brief instructions to the performer as the following:

- to whom the character is speaking

  ```
  (to John)
  ```

  ```
  (into phone)
  ```

  ```
  (to himself)
  ```

- a particular gesture or mannerism

  ```
  (raising his wine glass)
  ```

  ```
  (looking at her watch)
  ```

- how the dialogue is to be spoken

  ```
  (angry)
  ```

  ```
  (coughing)
  ```

  ```
  (softly)
  ```

  ```
  (a thick German accent)
  ```

Writing Parentheticals

There are several conventions for writing parentheticals:

- Because parentheticals are limited to words and phrases, they are never sentences and therefore never begin with a capital letter or end with a period.

  It is correct to write

  ```
  (loudly)
  ```

  But it would be incorrect to write it as

  ```
  (LOUDLY)
  ```

  ```
  (Loudly)
  ```

  ```
  (Loudly.)
  ```

- No more than two directions should be included in any parenthetical. If two directions appear, they should be separated by a semi-colon:

  ```
  (to the class; loudly)
  ```

- If the parenthetical requires more than a single line of type, the second line should be indented to align with the first.

  ```
                      EVANS
          That.
                  (pointing to the front of
                  his shirt)
          And these damned studs.  You'd think
          someone would invent a shirt stud that
          didn't require four hands to install.
  ```

WARNING:

Parentheticals are intended to be brief. Occasionally, however, you'll need to be more complex than a word or two can convey.

However, parentheticals that occupy more than a single line look unsightly. Whenever possible, avoid multiple lines for parentheticals.

Three Special Cases

While the use of a parenthetical is usually a judgment call, there are three special cases:

- a (beat),
- a (pause),
- an (interrupting)

(beat)

The parenthetical (beat) can have a variety of meanings. During a character's dialogue, it is most frequently used to

- indicate a change of thought
- suggest a moment of indecision
- convey a dramatic effect

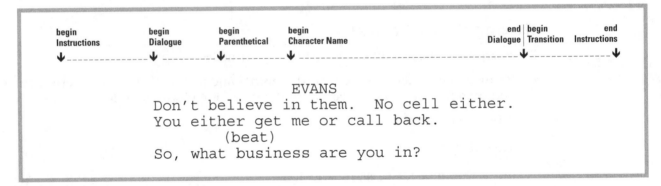

Aftershock, p. 10. In this example, the (beat) is used as Evans hesitates while changing the subject.

(interrupting)

This parenthetical indicates that the dialogue begun by the previous character is being interrupted by the current character.

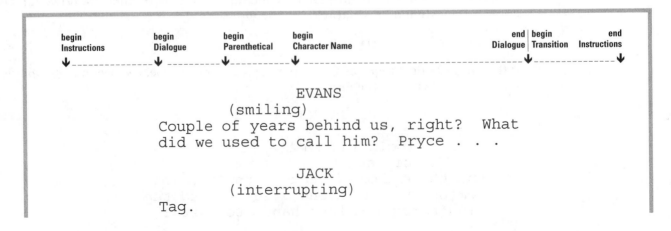

> EVANS
> Yes. "Pryce tag." I can't believe how
> stupid that sounds after all these years.

Aftershock, p. 5. The ellipsis at the end of Evans's sentence indicates that it is not complete; Jack finishes the sentence for Evans.

A VARIATION:

The parenthetical (overlapping) instructs the actors to "step on" each other's dialogue:

> JIM
> You set me up, trying to get me killed!

> GREG
> (overlapping)
> It's your own fault for being there!

The (overlapping) parenthetical indicates that both Jim and Greg are speaking their dialogue at very nearly the same time.

Although related, (overlapping) is not the same as (interrupting):

- Use (interrupting) to show that one character's dialogue is halted by the interruption of another character's dialogue.

- Use (overlapping) to show that two (or more) characters are simultaneously and continuously speaking their dialogue, allowing no interval for listening.

(pause)

The (pause) parenthetical signifies that a break in the dialogue occurs. This is most often used during telephone conversations.

For example, a character we see is speaking into the phone, but we do not hear the other end of the conversation. The (pause) indicates the lapse of time required for the other person's response.

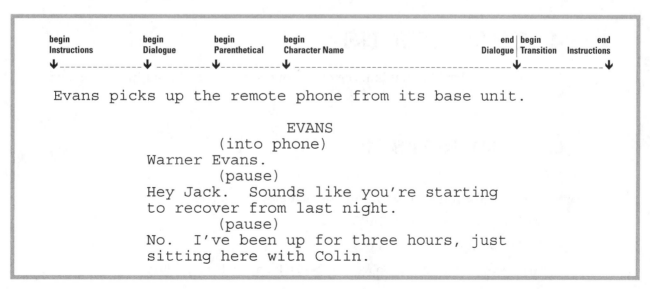

Aftershock, p. 10.

A VARIATION:

If a (pause) is used to indicate waiting time for a respondent, you could also use a (listening), as in

```
                    EVANS
               (into phone)
          Warner Evans.
               (listening)
          Hey Jack.  Sounds like you're starting
          to recover from last night.
               (listening)
          No.  I've been up for three hours, just
          sitting here with Colin.
```

Whichever convention you use, you must use it consistently.

Whether to Use (beat) or (pause)

These two parentheticals are often treated as interchangeable; however, they really have quite different applications:

- A (pause) is used primarily to indicate the listening interval during a phone conversation. It does not suggest any change in tone or emotion.

- A (beat) typically refers to the psychological or emotional context of a conversation.

Whether to Write a Parenthetical or an Instruction

There is a fundamental difference between using a parenthetical and an instruction as a device to deliver information:

- Basic cues to the speaker about the dialogue are contained in *parentheticals*, and these cues are limited to individual words and brief phrases. This better maintains the pace of the dialogue.

- Activities that affect the scene must be incorporated into the *instructions*.

4. TRANSITIONS

Transitions are bridges that link the end of one scene to the beginning of the next scene.

GENERAL RULES

Transitions

- are ALWAYS indented 6 $^1/_2$" from the left side of the page

- MUST be written in ALL CAPS

- MUST be punctuated by a colon

- are separated from text above and below by a single blank line

Every scene except the last MUST conclude with a transition to the next scene.

CUT TO:

This is the most common transition. It indicates an immediate change from one scene to the next.

- A CUT TO: occurs when the last frame of one scene is followed immediately by the first frame of the next scene.

  NOTE:

  For members of the production team (especially the editor), cuts occur between shots within a scene. However, for a screenplay, a cut is used *only* between scenes.

- If no transition is specified, it is assumed that the transition is a CUT TO:.

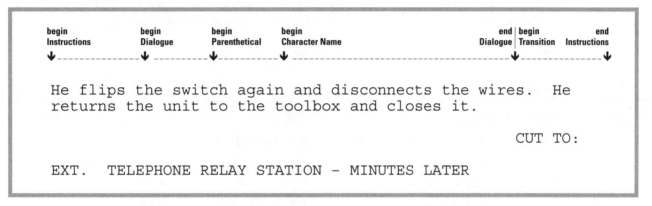

Aftershock, pp. 1–2.

There are occasions when a different kind of transition is called for.

DISSOLVE TO:

The DISSOLVE TO: is a more powerful means to bridge scenes than the CUT TO:.

- The DISSOLVE TO: is an optical technique whereby the last image of the previous scene fades out while the first image of the subsequent scene fades in. The two images overlap for a time.

- The DISSOLVE TO: implies a stronger connective relationship between scenes than a straight CUT TO:. Depending on context, a dissolve might imply simultaneous action or a significant time lapse; it also might suggest a linkage between specific characters or events.

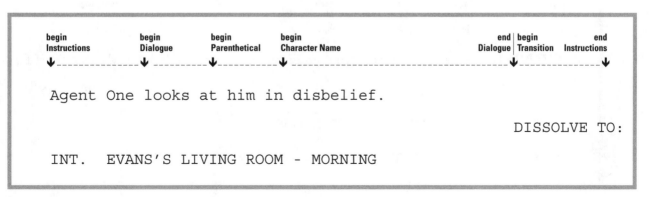

Aftershock, pp. 8–9.

FADE OUT:

The most powerful transitional device is the FADE OUT:.

- It indicates that the final image of one scene should gradually lose definition as the screen turns to black.

- The FADE OUT: is so powerful because it disrupts the continuous flow of images and stops—absolutely stops—the film. When used properly, it can be extremely effective.

  The fade typically indicates a significant jump in time. This jump is usually forward (omitting unnecessary time) but sometimes can be backward (as in a flashback).

- Because ending a scene with a FADE OUT: indicates a screen without an image, a FADE IN: is required to introduce the first image of the next scene.

Because the fade is so powerful, it must be used sparingly.

A VARIATION:

Instead of using the FADE OUT:/FADE IN: convention, you could use a FADE TO:.

Once again, the choice represents the degree of significance:

- Using the FADE OUT:/FADE IN: requires five lines on the page, but it provides a major break for the reader.

- Using the FADE TO: occupies three lines and places the transition on the same spatial level as the CUT TO: and DISSOLVE TO:.

If you are using numerous fades, it is probably best to use the FADE TO: form.

SCENES, SEQUENCES, AND TRANSITIONS

In the structure of a screenplay, a *scene* can be defined as beginning with a scene line and ending with a transition. Therefore, a scene is contained within a definable location and time.

In Part One, we have used a written transition to separate each scene, such as

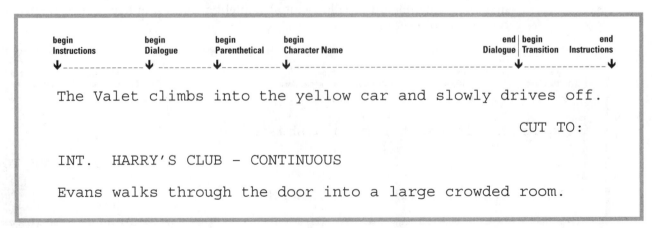

Aftershock, p. 3.

The Current Practice

Up to this point in Part One, writing each transition has been done to reinforce the convention that a transition (usually a CUT TO:) exists between each scene. However, the current practice in screenwriting has modified this practice.

Scenes and Transitions

In recent years, screenwriters have adopted a space-saving practice that affects the traditional way transitions have been applied to the screenwriting format:

- The convention of following the last line of a scene with a blank line, a transition, and then another blank line before the next scene line has almost entirely disappeared.

- The current convention has the advantage of reducing the number of lines between the scenes of a sequence from three to two. In other words, two blank lines are used to separate the scenes.

  This does not mean that the transitions are not present. But instead of writing them, it is understood that the transitions are present.

The previous example from *Aftershock* would now be written as

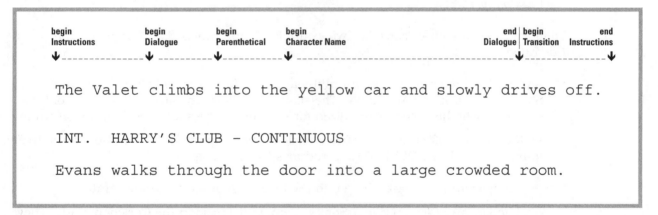

Aftershock, p. 3. This example has been modified from the original to omit the transition.

Over the course of a feature-length screenplay (approximately 110 pages), saving a single line between scenes could allow for adding another page or two for the story.

VERY IMPORTANT:

This only applies to the CUT TO: transition between scenes. If a DISSOLVE TO: or FADE TO: is used, then it must be written into the screenplay.

Sequences and Transitions

Even though the current practice eliminates adding the transitions between scenes, it retains adding the transitions between the *episodes*, called *sequences*, of a film.

- Before proceeding to explain this process, it is necessary to explain what a sequence is and how to recognize it.

- A *sequence* is composed of a series of closely related scenes that collectively complete a unified episode, with its own beginning, middle, and ending.

It may be helpful to think of sequences by their popular and recognizable forms. For example, there are

- *fight sequences*, such as the shootout between Will Kane and the Frank Miller gang in *High Noon* and Sean Thornton's marathon fist fight with Red Will Danaher over Mary Kate Danaher's dowry in *The Quiet Man*.

- *romantic sequences*, such as the love-making interlude in a French Riviera hotel suite between John Robie and Francie Stevens against the spectacular background of a fireworks display in *To Catch a Thief*.

- *suspense sequences*, such as Devlin's daring rescue of the incapacitated Alicia, which ends the Nazi conspiracy in *Notorious*.

- *chase sequences*, such as Indiana Jones racing to catch and capture the truck carrying the Ark of the Covenant, which the Nazis have stolen, in the centerpiece of *Raiders of the Lost Ark* and the usually dangerous and destructive vehicle chases through the city streets in *The French Connection*, *The Terminator*, and *The Matrix*.

- *dramatic sequences*, such as Jefferson Smith's filibuster before Congress in *Mr. Smith Goes to Washington*.

- *character sequences*, such as the flashback to Paris when Rick and Ilsa, deeply in love, plan to leave by train before the approaching German army invades the city in *Casablanca*.

To make this more clear, consider two examples from Francis Ford Coppola's *The Godfather:*

- A pivotal sequence occurs about mid-way in the film, when Michael kills Virgil Sollozzo and Captain McClusky. The sequence follows the attempted killing of Vito Corleone, who has been hospitalized for the injuries he sustained from bullet wounds.

As the music shifts from the tense chords of the hospital into a variation of the theme music, a slow DISSOLVE TO: introduces the next sequence.

> Michael and Clemenza drive into the heavily guarded Corleone estate.
>
> Michael and Clemenza join Sonny, Tom, and Tessio in the Corleone study. They discuss the peace meeting that Sollozzo has proposed, and Michael presents his plan to kill Sollozzo and McClusky at the meeting.
>
> Clemenza instructs Michael in the procedure to make the killing. In the Corleone dining room, Michael, Sonny, Tom, and the rest wait for Sonny's informant to reveal where the meeting will take place.
>
> Sollozzo and McClusky pick up Michael at Jack Dempsey's Restaurant and drive to Louis's Restaurant.
>
> At Louis's, Michael assassinates Sollozzo and McClusky.

The sequence ends with a long DISSOLVE TO:, as the music quickly shifts from the tension of the killing to a melodic theme while the consequences of the shooting are shown in a series of shots depicting the ensuing mob wars.

- The beginning of *The Godfather* contains an example of two sequences that are combined, or *intercut*. The first of these sequences takes place in the study of Don Vito Corleone's estate as he confers with a series of supplicants, each of whom wants a favor from him. The second sequence, occurring at the same time, shows the lavish wedding reception for his daughter, Connie, taking place on the lawn outside.

As the opening credits end, the film FADES IN: to the first image.

In his study, Don Corleone hears Bonasera (a mortician) ask for "justice" for the disfigurement inflicted on his daughter.

Outside at the reception, Vito refuses to have the family photograph taken without Michael. Sonny is angry at the FBI for taking photographs and getting the license numbers of the many guests.

Back in the study, another supplicant, Enzo (a baker), asks to have his daughter's boyfriend relocated from Italy to America.

Back at the reception, Michael (in his army uniform) appears with his girlfriend, Kay.

Back in the study, Luca Brasi pays his respects to the Don.

Back at the reception, Mrs. Corleone and others dance and sing.

Back in the study, the Don and Tom talk business.

Back at the reception, Johnny Fontaine, a popular crooner, enters to a loud ovation and starts singing.

Back in the study, Johnny asks the Don to get him a significant part in a Hollywood movie.

Back at the reception, a huge wedding cake is brought in.

Back in the study, the Don sends Tom to Hollywood. Tom mentions a meeting with Sollozzo.

Back at the reception, the family photograph is taken. Vito dances with Connie. FADE OUT:.

Both sequences could have been separated, but by intercutting the two, director Coppola juxtaposes the dual sides of the film's theme—the business of power and the bonding of family.

Although there are many variations on the structure of sequences, they all have certain characteristics:

- The events in a sequence are perceived as continuous, although there can be brief jumps in time to eliminate non-essential details.

- A sequence can be intercut with another sequence or other sequences to relate parallel situations.

- Sequences are usually separated by more powerful transitions than a simple CUT TO:—typically, a DISSOLVE TO: or FADE OUT:.

These transitions signal the reader that one episode has concluded and that another is about to begin.

PUTTING IT ALL TOGETHER

When you've finished writing the screenplay, you must add a few finishing touches before sending it off for consideration. These formatting procedures should not be done until you're ready to prepare the final version of your screenplay.

PAGE BREAKS

Ideally, a page should end with the transition from one scene to the next. That ideal, however, is seldom realized in formatting a screenplay.

- The next best alternative is to break a page on the blank line that follows a block of instruction or dialogue.

- Within the range of four or five lines, it is acceptable to have uneven amounts of white space at the bottom of a page to accommodate logical page breaks.

Breaking the Page in the Middle of a Block of Instructions

If a block of instructions is too lengthy to fit on the page, then you must divide it:

- The first option is to find a logical place to break the single paragraph block into two separate blocks and then to break the page on the blank line that separates the blocks.

- If the first option is not available, then you must end the page with no fewer than two lines of type and carry the remainder over to the next page. You must be certain that at least two lines of type appear at the top of the next page, as well.

Nothing is more unsightly on the page of a screenplay than messy page breaks.

Breaking the Page Within a Dialogue-Block

When a block of dialogue is too lengthy to fit on a page, then you must carry it over to the next page, This requires using the (MORE) (CONT'D) convention.

If the bottom of one page is

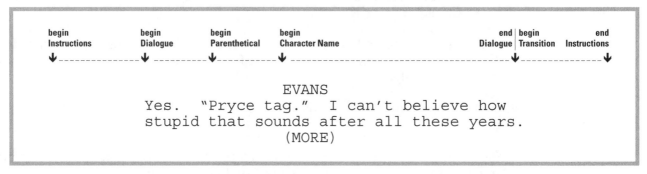

Aftershock, p. 5.

then the top of the next page would be

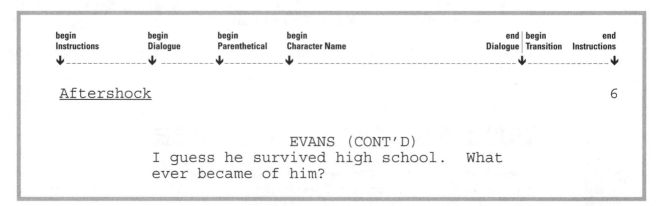

Aftershock, p. 6.

The (MORE) means that there is more of the dialogue on the next page. The (CONT'D) is an abbreviation for continued.

The (MORE)/(CONT'D) Convention

- ALWAYS write (MORE) and (CONT'D) in caps, and ALWAYS enclose each term in parentheses. In addition,
- The (MORE) ALWAYS appears as the final line of the page and uses the same left indent setting as the character-name.
- The (CONT'D) ALWAYS appears on the top line of the next page following the re-identification of the character-name.
- Both the (MORE) and the (CONT'D) are part of the dialogue-block and therefore not separated from the other components by a blank line.

FIRST NOTE:
The break should occur *between* two sentences, rather than truncate a sentence.

SECOND NOTE:
This use of (CONT'D) is not to be confused with the (cont'd) discussed previously.

THIRD NOTE:
The adjustment of dialogue and instructions to accommodate clean page breaks should be done only when the screenplay is considered finished and ready for submission.

UNACCEPTABLE PAGE BREAKS

Just as it is unacceptable to have justified (even) right margins in a screenplay, it is unacceptable to break passages of instructions or dialogue at certain points.

In Instructions

- NEVER allow less than two lines of a block of instructions at the bottom or top of a page. It is better to alter the bottom page margin a few lines to accommodate a natural break (or at least a reasonable break) in the text.
- NEVER end a page with a scene line. When the end of the page contains space enough for a transition and the scene line for the next scene, end the page with the transition and bump the scene line to the top of the following page.

In Dialogue

- NEVER break a dialogue-block between the character-name, the parenthetical (if any), and the first few lines of the dialogue.
- NEVER carry less than two lines of dialogue over to the next page.
- Although the (MORE)/(CONT'D) device is available, avoid it whenever possible.

A WARNING:
Your screenplay will look and read much better if you either shorten or extend the page a bit to try to make the dialogue fit together rather than use this device for only a couple lines of dialogue.

You should break dialogue only when a lengthy passage will not fit on the same page.

SCENE NUMBERS

In many professional screenplays, you will see a series of sequential numbers to identify each scene line, such as

```
12.   INT.   JOHN'S KITCHEN - DAY                    12.
```

Scene numbers are added when a screenplay is being prepared for production. They should never be included in a screenplay that is just being submitted for consideration.

THE TITLE PAGE

The title page consists of five elements, all typed in 12-point Courier.

1. The *title* is centered on the page, approximately 16 spaces down from the top. It is typed in ALL CAPS and underlined.

2. The phrase *an original screenplay* is centered on the page, three spaces down from the title; it is typed in lower case.

3. The word *by* is centered on the page, three spaces down from "an original screenplay"; it is also in lower case.

4. The *writer's name* is centered on the page, three spaces down from "by." It is typed in the normal manner with initial caps for all words.

   If more than one author is being credited, the second name should follow the first after a comma and a letter space. The order of the listing should be by mutual consent or alphabetical.

5. *Contact information* is flush with the left margin, six to eight spaces up from the bottom of the page.

   NOTE:

   The contact person should be whoever is representing the property.

   Initially, this would be the writer. If an agent has been secured, the contact person will be the agent and a new title page will be typed. If the screenplay is optioned, the contact person will change again to the producer or the production company.

A Few Things You Don't Want on the Title Page

• NEVER place a date on the screenplay.

• NEVER use any kind of artwork or elaborate type. Keep it plain and simple.

• NEVER include any prefatory or introductory material. Let the screenplay speak for itself.

• NEVER place information about registration (with the Writers Guild) or copyright (with the U.S. government). It is assumed that you know to do this.

   In fact, indicating information about registration or copyright on the title page (or cover) betrays a lack of professionalism on the part of the screenwriter.

   This does not mean that you should not protect your screenplay. You do need to register or copyright your property.

An example of a title page appears on the next page.

AFTERSHOCK

an original screenplay

by

Stephen E. Bowles, Ronald Mangravite & Peter A. Zorn, Jr.

Contact:

Name
Address
Telephone
e-mail

FINAL TOUCHES

Refer back to the beginning of Part One for some additional information on preparing your screenplay for submission. Important restrictions on duplicating, binding, and covering your screenplay are cited there.

PROTECTION OF SCREENPLAYS

Prior to submission to agents, producers, readers, and the like, every screenplay should be registered with either the Writers Guild of America, West, or the U.S. Copyright Office.

For more information, contact:

Writers Guild of America, West, Inc.
Intellectual Property Registry
7000 West Third Street
Los Angeles, CA 90048-4329
Telephone: 323-782-4500
Fax: 323-782-4803
Website: www.wga.org

Library of Congress
Copyright Office
101 Independence Avenue SE
Washington, DC 20559-6000
Telephone: 202-707-3000
Website: www.copyright.gov

PART TWO

Advanced Format and Style

Audiences don't know somebody sits down and writes a picture. They think the actors make it up as they go along.

From *Sunset Boulevard* (1950)
Screenplay by Billy Wilder,
Charles Brackett, and
D. M. Marshman, Jr.

NOTE:

In Part One, every scene was separated from every other scene by a transition.

To provide the reader of a screenplay with a stronger sense of the sequential building within the narrative, the popular trend is to preserve the unity of sequences by

- eliminating the CUT TO: transitions between the scenes within a sequence but
- retaining the CUT TO:, DISSOLVE TO:, and FADE OUT:/FADE IN: transitions between sequences.

In Part Two, we will adhere to the current practice of omitting the CUT TO: transitions (replaced by two blank lines) between scenes.

The information provided in Part One addresses the basic procedures of format and style and can be used to write a complete screenplay. As you progress as a screenwriter, however, you will encounter narrative situations that require techniques that go beyond the basic procedures of Part One.

Part Two solves more complicated problems. Often, the solutions will cross the line between format and style.

What is *style?* Style is usually associated with a distinctive or characteristic quality that separates the interesting from the ordinary. One commonly thinks of a literary style, an architectural style, a personality style, or a directorial style.

Style in screenwriting is not "writing style" in the way Hemingway described the sunrise over the mountains of Africa. Rather, it is a combination of narrative and technique that compels the reader to experience the screenplay in his or her imagination as the movie would progress on the screen.

Enhancing the Narrative

Remember, the *look* and *read* of a screenplay are what invites the reader into your story.

- To achieve the goal of making the screenplay read as it would appear on the screen, you may need to bend, stretch, or even break some established procedures and conventions.

- But be careful! Too much tampering with the accepted format can easily backfire and alienate an otherwise receptive reader.

Providing the reader with a sense of the story's *pacing* is an elusive but important element in the writing style of an effective screenplay.

- Pacing addresses the "adrenaline flow"—how the rhythm quickens or slows to accommodate the needs of the story.

- High-voltage action scenes are best written in a rapid-fire style. You don't want to slow the momentum by using complicated sentences or lengthy instructions. On the other hand, tender romantic interludes may need a more casual and unhurried style.

In this sense, you're not writing a *screenplay,* you're writing a *movie.* And you must think of it as a *movie*—something that has a look as well as a story.

In addition to pacing, the way the instructions are written allows the screenwriter a large amount of control over the film's *look.* Although you cannot call for specific camera set-ups, you can manipulate the wording of instructions to translate as visuals.

- If you write that a character's eyes are bloodshot, how else could it be filmed other than as a close-up? If you write about the vast expanse of a desert, it would need to be done as a long shot.

- Remember, there is very little that you can imagine that can't be accomplished in motion pictures. So, if you think a visual is important to your narrative, then you should describe it the way you imagine it. Someone will find a way to make it happen.

Many techniques are available to help create the pace and look you want the reader to experience. That is what Part Two is all about.

All about Slug Lines

THE MASTER SHOT

In Part One, each scene was written as a *master shot.* This means that each scene was written as though the camera were recording the entire scene in a single continuous shot that includes everything you can see and hear within the range of the location as defined in the scene line. The master shot is the most basic way to construct a scene.

SLUG LINES

On occasion, you will need to isolate or identify a particular person, place, object, sound, effect, view, or activity within a given scene. *Slug lines* call attention to specific details.

- The use of slug lines provides a flexible and powerful technique for a screenwriter to control the dramatic impact of a scene.
- However, slug lines must be applied sparingly. They are not to be used just because they are available, and too many of them will hamper the reading.

Formatting Slug Lines

Slug lines

- are ALWAYS typed in ALL CAPS
- conform to the same margins as the scene line and the instructions
- are ALWAYS separated from other elements by a blank line above and below them

Slug lines look similar to scene lines and, in many respects, they function as miniature scene lines. Slug lines are also like instructions; they describe the progress of the scene.

How Slug Lines Work

Consider the following example. which is written using the basic format of Part One:

```
EXT.   CITY STREET, INDUSTRIAL AREA - NIGHT

It is raining.  A large truck with a strapped-down load of
pipes is being followed closely by a new Mercedes.


INT.   TRUCK - CONTINUOUS

The Driver is not paying attention to the road.  His interest
is on trying to roll a cigarette rather than driving.


INT.   MERCEDES - CONTINUOUS

Benny is dialing on a cell phone while looking for an
opportunity to pass the truck.
```

In the back seat, Gudge is holding a pistol on Jason whose head is down, his wrists bound by cord.

Benny puts down the phone.

> BENNY
> (to Gudge)
> Remove all his identification before
> we make him disappear.

Jason opens his eyes but does not move. Gudge switches his pistol to the other hand and goes through Jason's pockets.

INT. TRUCK - CONTINUOUS

The Driver spills his tobacco all over his lap. As he looks down to scrape it up, he inadvertently swerves the truck.

EXT. CITY STREET, INDUSTRIAL AREA - CONTINUOUS

The swerving truck sideswipes the Mercedes, knocking it into a guard rail.

Explanation and Notes

In the preceding example, there are three separate locations: (1) the city street with the truck and the Mercedes, (2) the inside of the truck where the Driver's action takes place, and (3) the inside of the Mercedes with Benny, Gudge, and Jason. This version takes five separate scenes.

Now consider the following revision:

EXT./INT. CITY STREET/THE TRUCK/THE MERCEDES - NIGHT

It is raining. A large truck with a strapped-down load of pipes is being followed closely by a new Mercedes.

INSIDE THE TRUCK -

the Driver is not paying attention to the road. His interest is on trying to roll a cigarette rather than driving.

INSIDE THE MERCEDES -

Benny is dialing on a cell phone, while looking for an opportunity to pass the truck.

In the back seat, Gudge is guarding Jason who is unconscious.
Jason's head is down, his wrists bound by cord.

Benny puts down the phone.

                          BENNY
                    (to Gudge)
          Remove all his identification before
          we make him disappear.

Jason opens his eyes but does not move. Gudge switches his
pistol to the other hand and goes through Jason's pockets.

INSIDE THE TRUCK -

the Driver spills his tobacco all over his lap. As he looks
down to scrape it up, he inadvertently swerves the truck.

THE CITY STREET

The swerving truck sideswipes the Mercedes, knocking it into
a guard rail.

FIRST NOTE:

The above example uses an *expanded scene line*

    EXT./INT. CITY STREET/THE TRUCK/THE MERCEDES - NIGHT

incorporating the three separate locations into a single, unified scene.

- EXT./INT. tells the reader that the scene will use both exterior and interior set-ups.
- CITY STREET/THE TRUCK/THE MERCEDES indicates that the scene will include three different locations.

The expanded scene line has the advantage of giving the scene more unity by keeping all the action under a single scene line, thus reading more like it would play in the movie.

SECOND NOTE:

Whenever appropriate, a smoother reading is created when a slug line is integrated into the grammatical unity of a sentence of instruction.

- The use of a *dash* at the end of an instruction or slug line indicates that whatever follows is a continuation of a sentence. For example:

    MARY -

    watches John in amazement.

- Following the dash, the first word of the next line begins with a lower case letter.
- The absence of a dash indicates that each is self-contained.

    THE CITY STREET

Three Types of Slug Lines

Although all slug lines are similar in appearance, they can function quite differently. At their most basic, slug lines fall into three categories:

- utility slug lines
- visual slug lines
- non-visual slug lines

Because slug lines provide the screenwriter with such a diverse range of applications, it is necessary to understand what each type does and how it is formatted.

WHAT UTILITY SLUG LINES DO

There are four fundamental applications for this type of slug line. Utility slug lines can be used:

- to return from a restricted view to the master shot

  RETURN TO SCENE

- to replace a series of specific slug lines with a general one

  INTERCUT AS NEEDED

- to visually identify a particular locale

  ESTABLISHING - SAN FRANCISCO

- to indicate words that are superimposed over the image on the screen

  SUPER IN/OUT - "MIAMI, 1958"

WHAT VISUAL SLUG LINES DO

Visual slug lines function to restrict the open view of the master shot.

- Although they are not actual camera directions (such as calling for a close-up or a two shot), they convey a specific view of a situation.
- While in the specific view imposed by the slug line, you cannot refer to any other visual activity outside the slug line.

Slug lines that draw our visual attention to something particular within the master shot can be used for such diverse purposes as the following:

- to isolate a character or object within the scene

  JOHN

  ON JOHN

  THE BOMB

  THE DESKTOP

- to temporarily leave or interrupt the scene

  ```
  JOHN'S P.O.V. - FROM KITCHEN TO YARD OUTSIDE
  ```

  ```
  CUTAWAY - MOVING CAR
  ```

- to replace a scene (and scene line) with a substitute

  ```
  SERIES OF SHOTS - CAMPUS LIFE
  ```

  ```
  INSERT - MAP OF TIBET
  ```

- to subdivide a scene into differing activities, to subdivide a multi-room structure into specific rooms, and to combine multi-rooms into a single scene line

Dialogue While in a Visual Slug Line

- With a visual slug line, you can have characters who are on-screen (that is, within the visual range specified by the slug line) speaking in the normal manner.
- If, however, you include dialogue by characters who are not in the view defined by the slug line, then that dialogue would be considered off-screen (O.S.).

Terminating Visual Slug Lines

With a visual slug line, you are *always* in the view imposed by the slug line *until* you

- RETURN TO SCENE, which would take the view back to the master shot
- call for another visual slug line, which shifts the view
- end the scene with a transition

WHAT NON-VISUAL SLUG LINES DO

Unlike visual slug lines, non-visual slug lines do NOT affect the view, as defined by the master shot.

Like visual slug lines, non-visual slug lines have diverse applications. Non-visual slug lines can be used for these purposes:

- to indicate a lapse of time

  ```
  LATER
  ```

  ```
  SEVERAL HOURS LATER
  ```

- to identify a critical sound

  ```
  THUNDER
  ```

  ```
  A GUNSHOT
  ```

- to emphasize something dramatic

  ```
  SUDDENLY
  ```

Terminating Non-Visual Slug Lines

Because non-visual slug lines have no affect on the master shot, they do not require any termination.

Non-visual slug lines are usually followed by instructions, which describe the *effects* of the slug line.

IMPORTANT:

A distinction is made between *visual slug lines* and *non-visual slug lines* because of the different ways in which they affect the scene.

- Slug lines that direct our visual attention to a particular aspect of the scene requires a means of terminating that view.

- Slug lines that are non-visual do not require any termination because they function independently of the master view of the scene.

Utility Slug Lines

RETURN TO SCENE

To get back to the master shot from any visual slug line, you use another slug line— RETURN TO SCENE. The slug line RETURN TO SCENE refers to the master shot as defined by the scene line.

```
INT.   COLLEGE CLASSROOM - DAY

The students file into the room.

Professor Jones is standing, looking out the window.

PROFESSOR JONES' P.O.V. - LOOKING AT PARKING LOT

A circus CLOWN climbs out of a bright yellow Maserati
and slowly walks to the building entrance.

RETURN TO SCENE

Professor Jones shakes his head in disbelief, goes to the
blackboard and begins to write.
```

Explanation and Notes

In this example, the *master shot* would encompass the whole of the scene's location (COLLEGE CLASSROOM). As the students file into the room, our visual attention then shifts from Professor Jones at the window (part of the master shot) to what Professor Jones sees (his P.O.V.) as he looks out the window.

From this, it is necessary to get out of Professor Jones's view and return to the master shot. RETURN TO SCENE accomplishes this. Professor Jones goes to the blackboard and the scene continues.

VARIATIONS:

Instead of RETURN TO SCENE, you could use either of two equally acceptable alternatives to get back to the master shot:

- BACK TO SCENE means exactly the same as RETURN TO SCENE.

  ```
  A circus CLOWN climbs out of a bright yellow Maserati
  and slowly walks to the building entrance.

  BACK TO SCENE

  Professor Jones shakes his head in disbelief, goes to the
  blackboard and begins to write.
  ```

- BACK TO (the scene line location), which in the above example would be

  ```
  A circus CLOWN climbs out of a bright yellow Maserati
  and slowly walks to the building entrance.

  BACK TO COLLEGE CLASSROOM

  Professor Jones shakes his head in disbelief, goes to the
  blackboard and begins to write.
  ```

ESTABLISHING

On occasion, it may be important to identify a generic or specific geographical location. The slug line ESTABLISHING allows the director to select an icon or series of images that clearly conveys that location.

For example:

```
ESTABLISHING - PARIS
```

and the director might use the Eiffel Tower

```
ESTABLISHING - THE MIDWEST
```

and the director might use a vast prairie landscape with grain silos or tractors in a field.

Common Applications

Establishing shots are commonly used in two basic situations:

- Most often, ESTABLISHING is used to introduce a geographical location.
- When the narrative shifts from one geographical location to another, such a slug line can be used as a segue.

Formatting

Although an establishing view is similar to a scene, it is *not* a scene; it is a slug line. Therefore:

- It follows the capping, line spacing, and margin settings of other slug lines.
- ESTABLISHING always refers to exteriors.
- A general time can be included:

```
ESTABLISHING - MOSCOW (NIGHT)
```

Terminating

A blank line separates the slug line from the following scene line. There is no transition.

```
ESTABLISHING - LOS ANGELES

INT.  A FASHIONABLE RESTAURANT - EVENING

The dinner CROWD is being seated and served.
```

Explanation and Notes

By using the ESTABLISHING slug line, you are telling the director that the following scene takes place in the city of Los Angeles. You are also informing the director that, for the narrative, it doesn't matter *how* it is established that the city is Los Angeles.

INTERCUT AS NEEDED

The slug line INTERCUT AS NEEDED is used to preserve the continuity of an action that occurs in diverse locations.

Common Applications

The slug line INTERCUT AS NEEDED is most commonly used in phone conversations when you want visual images of both sides of the conversation but it is not important which side is shown at any particular moment.

Advantages

If it is not critical which character is on screen during a phone conversation, the dialogue can be written as a continuous event. No instructions or slug lines are needed to break the flow of the conversation.

Formatting

An intercut follows the capping, line spacing, and margin settings of other slug lines.

- Begin with the instruction INTERCUT AS NEEDED.
- Follow it with a dash (separated by a character-space before and after).
- Then attach a brief notation that clarifies what is being intercut.

Terminating

When the conversation is finished, you have several options:

- RETURN TO SCENE to get back to the master shot.
- END INTERCUT, which would return to the location (identified in the scene line or slug line) where the intercut began.
- Use a transition (like CUT TO:), which would not only end the intercut but also end the scene.

A WARNING:

Unless there is a narrative reason to withhold such information, all locations used in the intercutting must be clearly identified. Use either:

- separate scenes to establish the locations and participants before the intercutting begins
- a single scene (with an expanded scene line) and slug lines to describe the locations and participants

---

INT.   DUDLEY'S HOTEL ROOM - NIGHT

Dudley is sitting at the desk with piles of paperwork on it.

The phone RINGS.   Dudley answers.

               DUDLEY
           (into phone)
     Hello.

               BECKY (V.O.)
           (over phone)
   Dudley, it's Becky.

INT.   DOWNTOWN BAR - CONTINUOUS

It's a lively, crowded place where Becky must lean into the pay phone to avoid the loud NOISE.

               BECKY
           (into phone)
   When did you get in?

               DUDLEY (V.O.)
           (over phone)
   About four.

INTERCUT AS NEEDED - BECKY AND DUDLEY ON PHONE

               BECKY
   I'm down here at Giovanni's with the
   gang. Why not come down and join us?

               DUDLEY
   I can be there in fifteen minutes.

               BECKY
   Great. We'll see you then.

END INTERCUT

Becky hangs up the phone.

Note: In this example, the phone exchange between Becky and Dudley is very short. Normally, with an INTERCUT AS NEEDED instruction, the exchange would be longer.

Explanation and Notes

By specifying an INTERCUT AS NEEDED, you are informing the director that during the phone conversation between Becky and Dudley, it is not important to the narrative which character is on screen at any given time.

For a phone conversation:

- Adding the information BECKY AND DUDLEY ON PHONE to the slug line eliminates the need to repeat the parenthetical (into phone) each time Becky and Dudley speak. But all the dialogue that follows this instruction must be spoken into the telephone.

- If, however, Becky or Dudley were to speak to someone else during the phone conversation, then you would *not* include the information ON PHONE in the slug line. And the parentheticals (into phone) *must* be included each time Becky and Dudley speak into the phone.

SUPERIMPOSED WORDS

The term SUPER IN/OUT is movie shorthand for *superimposition* of words that appear briefly over the image on the screen and then disappear.

Common Applications

Most frequently, supers are used to provide information to the audience about such matters as

- where the scene is set
- when it is taking place
- the names of characters
- what has happened just before the scene begins

Formatting

As a slug line, superimpositions have two components:

- the term SUPER IN/OUT followed by a dash (separated by a character-space before and after)
- the words that are to appear over the image include quotation marks

```
SUPER IN/OUT - "MIAMI BEACH, 1946"

SUPER IN/OUT - "THE CONSOLIDATED STAR CRUISER ENIGMA"
```

Like all slug lines, supers should be used only when absolutely necessary.

Terminating

Because the visual component of the scene is not interrupted, no termination is required for a superimposition.

```
EXT.  MIAMI BEACH - DAY

The bright sun accents the deco surfaces of the architecture.
To the ocean side, hundreds of BATHERS are crowding the beach.

SUPER IN/OUT - "MIAMI BEACH, 1946"

Walking down the sidewalk is JACK SLADER, late twenties,
ruggedly handsome, dressed in a white suit and a Panama hat.
```

Explanation and Notes

- In this example, since the crowded beaches and deco architecture of Miami Beach still exist today (and don't necessarily define the time period), it is important to clearly state the time "1946" directly. The SUPER does this.

- The quotation marks that flank the superimposed words don't appear in the text that appears on screen. The quotation marks are only used in the screenplay to set off the text from the instructions.

Visual Slug Lines

ISOLATING CHARACTERS AND OBJECTS

Most visual slug lines are used to direct the viewer's attention to a specific character or object within the scene.

By isolating a character or object with a slug line, you are modifying the master shot and informing the reader that *this* is important.

Formatting

With a visual slug line, you only need to specify the character or object of our visual attention. It may take a typical form, such as

```
MARCIE

THE COMPUTER SCREEN
```

Or it could include more than a single character or object, as in

```
JOHN AND MARY

THE GROUP AT THE TABLE

THE CROWD
```

Use of BACK TO

Once identified in the scene through an initial slug line, those characters or objects can be re-identified through the use of another slug line, BACK TO. For example:

BACK TO MARCIE

BACK TO THE COMPUTER SCREEN

BACK TO THE GAME

This would remind the reader that you are returning back to an image that has already been established.

Terminating

Because a character or object slug line re-defines the master shot, you need to conclude the view in one of these ways:

• with a RETURN TO SCENE to get back to the master shot

• with another slug line that re-defines the master shot

• with a transition that ends the scene

INT.   CONFERENCE ROOM - DAY

Seated around the conference table are Arne Schmidt, Jack Davis, and Connie Blankenship.

At the head of the table, Marcie Andrews is standing at a large easel making a presentation.

MARCIE -

is turning the page.

                        MARCIE
                   (to the group)
          As you all can see, guest satisfaction
          numbers are down significantly from
          last quarter. This is due in . . .

Marcie drones on as -

SCHMIDT -

who is barely listening, makes notes on a legal pad.

DAVIS -

scrolls information on his laptop computer.

THE COMPUTER SCREEN

A video game of solitaire appears. Cards are moved around.

```
BACK TO MARCIE

She flips another page.

RETURN TO SCENE
```

Explanation and Notes

In this scene, the action takes place in the conference room, and our attention is directed around the room from character to character, each isolated by a slug line. This technique enables the writer to make suggestions about the personality of each participant.

POINT-OF-VIEW (P.O.V.)

A point-of-view (always abbreviated as P.O.V.) refers to the *field of vision*, as perceived by a specific character.

- The P.O.V. provides a means to temporarily isolate and describe the object of a particular character's visual attention at a given moment.

- Use a P.O.V. only when it provides essential narrative or character information that serves the development of the screenplay.

Common Applications

Using a P.O.V. can make it absolutely clear that a character is seeing something particular and that the viewer knows the character is seeing it.

The P.O.V. is a character's view of something

- *within* the view of the master shot of the scene

- *outside* the boundaries of the master shot

Regardless of whether the object of the P.O.V. is inside or outside the master shot, you can *only* describe what the observing character can see from the P.O.V.

Formatting

The P.O.V. is a particular kind of visual slug line:

- It is ALWAYS attached to *someone* or *something* in the scene and MUST be clearly identified as such.

  Most often, a P.O.V. belongs to a single person; however, it could also belong to a group, to an animal, or even to an unknown observer. In rare cases, a P.O.V. could also belong to an object.

  ```
  MARY'S P.O.V.

  DOG'S P.O.V.

  THE CROWD'S P.O.V.

  UNKNOWN P.O.V.
  ```

- This type of slug line is followed by a dash (separated by a character-space before and after) and then a brief description of what is being observed.

  Although it is often understood from the context, it is useful to indicate *from where to where* or *through what* the P.O.V. occurs.

  ```
  MARY'S P.O.V. - LOOKING AT THE CLOCK

  DOG'S P.O.V. - ACTIVITY ON THE STREET

  THE CROWD'S P.O.V. - THE SCOREBOARD

  UNKNOWN P.O.V. - THROUGH TELESCOPIC LENS
  ```

Terminating

Since every P.O.V. is a visual refinement of the master shot, it requires one of the following:

- a RETURN TO SCENE to get back to the master shot
- another slug line that gives a different view
- Although unusual, the P.O.V. could end with a transition.

Using a P.O.V. within the Scene

A P.O.V. is used within the scene when both the observer and observed are present within the boundaries defined by the scene line.

The P.O.V. may be within an interior location (usually relatively confined), as in this example:

```
INT.  PERSONNEL OFFICE - DAY

Henry enters the spacious room which looks less like an
office than a private study.  As instructed, he sits in the
cushioned chair across from the oversized desk . . . and
waits . . . and waits.

Henry begins to fidget and anxiously look around the room.
His eye catches something on the desktop.

HENRY'S P.O.V. - FOLDER ON DESK

It is a sealed manila envelope with his name clearly printed
on the outside.

RETURN TO SCENE

This is a surprise.  He nervously looks toward the entrance
door.
```

Explanation and Notes

In this situation, Henry is waiting to apply for a job. He is unaware that the company knows anything about him except his name. Seeing the manila folder with his name on it raises a series of disturbing questions and throws him into an anxious state.

A P.O.V. can also be set in an exterior (usually more expansive) scene:

```
EXT.  THE BATTLEFIELD - DAY

The squad halts at the bottom of a shallow ridge.  Lt.
Simpson gives a hand signal and the men silently sit and
rest.

LT. SIMPSON -

makes his way to the top of the ridge.  Positioning himself
behind a large fallen log, he raises his head up over the
log and surveys the opposite ridge.

He takes his binoculars and scans the area.

LT. SIMPSON'S P.O.V. - THE FAR RIDGE (THROUGH BINOCULARS)

On the opposite ridge, the enemy ENGINEERS are wiring
charges of explosives to the under-structure of a bridge.

BACK TO LT. SIMPSON -

as he lowers the binoculars and drops back down behind the
log.  He rolls into a crouch and scrambles down the hill.
```

Explanation and Notes

If we only need to know that Lt. Simpson is doing surveillance, we could simply see him looking through the binoculars in the master shot without any P.O.V. In this instance, however, it is important that we see what Lt. Simpson sees, so the P.O.V. convention is used to convey that visual information.

VARIATIONS:

In "The Battlefield" scene just examined, it is essential that the P.O.V. be seen through the binoculars. Therefore, this must be incorporated into the slug line. There are several ways to do this.

```
LT. SIMPSON'S P.O.V. - THE FAR RIDGE (THROUGH BINOCULARS)

LT. SIMPSON'S P.O.V. - THROUGH BINOCULARS - THE FAR RIDGE
```

or without the first dash as

```
LT. SIMPSON'S P.O.V. THROUGH BINOCULARS - THE FAR RIDGE
```

Most P.O.V. slug lines will only include whose point of view is being described and what is being seen. However, anything else that affects the P.O.V. must also be included in the slug line.

Using a P.O.V. Outside the Scene

This use of the P.O.V. occurs when the observer is *within* the location of the scene line but the object of the observation is *beyond* the range of the scene line.

Applying the P.O.V. device, you can temporarily break away from the master shot of the scene to an outside view. This device eliminates the need to write the outside P.O.V. as a separate scene, which would disrupt the flow of the scene.

Consider the following example:

```
INT.   STEVE AND DIANE'S BEDROOM - AFTERNOON

Steve is putting studs in the front of his pleated shirt
while across the room Diane is zipping up her evening gown.

Steve walks to the window and looks down.


EXT.   THE YARD - CONTINUOUS

Angie is playing on the swing.  She has twisted the chains
together and lets go, spinning faster and faster.


INT.   STEVE AND DIANE'S BEDROOM - CONTINUOUS

Steve turns to Diane.

                    STEVE
          Where's Lana?  Isn't she supposed
          to be watching Angie?

Diane joins Steve at the window.


EXT.   THE YARD - CONTINUOUS

The swing is empty, still spinning.  A blue van pulls out
of the driveway and speeds up the road.
```

Explanation and Notes

In this example, the numerous transitions and scene lines fragment the bedroom scene.

Now consider the following alternative:

```
INT.   STEVE AND DIANE'S BEDROOM - AFTERNOON

Steve is putting studs in the front of his pleated shirt
while across the room Diane is zipping up her evening gown.

Steve walks to the window and looks down.

STEVE'S P.O.V. - THROUGH WINDOW TO YARD BELOW

Angie is playing on the swing.  She has twisted the chains
together and lets go, spinning faster and faster.
```

```
RETURN TO SCENE

Steve turns to Diane.

                         STEVE
          Where's Lana?  Isn't she supposed
          to be watching Angie?

Diane joins Steve at the window.

STEVE AND DIANE'S P.O.V. - THROUGH WINDOW TO YARD BELOW

The swing is empty, still spinning.  A blue van pulls out
of the driveway and speeds up the road.
```

Explanation and Notes

In this version, the `P.O.V.` allows the screenwriter to preserve the flow of the scene in the bedroom while incorporating an activity outside the scene in the yard.

Including Dialogue in a P.O.V.

Using a `P.O.V.` places us in the line of sight of a character; its purpose is to allow us to see exactly what the character sees at that moment.

Although part of the character (usually the back or shoulder) may be visible, while in the `P.O.V.`, we cannot see the character's face.

- Therefore, any dialogue spoken by a character whose `P.O.V.` we share must be considered as spoken off-screen (`O.S.`).

- To omit the (`O.S.`) would be contradictory, indicating that we see both what the character sees and him speaking the dialogue.

```
INT.  JOHN'S LIVING ROOM - DAY

John and Nadine are sitting at the table.  He is nervous and
fidgety, having a difficult time keeping his coffee steady as
he raises the cup to take a sip.

He looks at the antique clock over the mantle.

JOHN'S P.O.V. - THE CLOCK

It shows 4:30.

                         JOHN (O.S.)
          It should have been here by now.

RETURN TO SCENE

                         NADINE
          I don't know why you're so upset.
```

```
From outside, a vehicle SCREECHES to a stop.

A look of panic overcomes John.  He quickly gets up--toppling
the chair in the process--and rushes to the window.

JOHN'S P.O.V. - FROM LIVING ROOM TO STREET

A FedEx truck is parked in front of the house.  The DRIVER
is walking toward the front door.

                    JOHN (O.S.)
                (relieved)
            Finally!

RETURN TO SCENE

John uses his sleeve to wipe the sweat from his brow.  He
rushes out the door.
```

Explanation and Notes

Since John's dialogue is contained within his P.O.V., it is written as off-screen (O.S.).

- While in John's first P.O.V., Nadine does not speak. Her dialogue occurs after we have returned to the master shot.

- If, however, Nadine had replied to John while in his P.O.V. as he looked out the window, then she would not be on screen and her dialogue would need to be (O.S.) as would John's. If that were the situation, then it would be written

```
JOHN'S P.O.V. - THE CLOCK

It shows 4:30.

                    JOHN (O.S.)
            It should have been here by now.

                    NADINE (O.S.)
            I don't know why you're so upset.

RETURN TO SCENE
```

- Alternatively, if John's P.O.V. included Nadine when she spoke, then her dialogue would not be (O.S.).

A VARIATION:

Because the time on the clock is so brief and specific, requiring no other description or information, it is possible to include the time in the slug line. For example:

```
JOHN'S P.O.V. - THE CLOCK (4:30)
```

Whether to Write the Situation as an Instruction, a Slug Line, or a P.O.V.

Take, for example, a basic context, in which John looks at a clock on the wall. This could be written in three different ways:

- as an instruction:

  ```
  John nervously looks at the clock on the wall.  It shows
  precisely 4:00.
  ```

- as a slug line:

  ```
  John nervously looks at the clock on the wall.

  THE CLOCK

  It shows precisely 4:00.

  RETURN TO SCENE
  ```

- as a P.O.V.:

  ```
  John nervously looks toward the wall.

  JOHN'S P.O.V. - CLOCK ON THE WALL

  The time is precisely 4:00.

  RETURN TO SCENE
  ```

These three examples all convey the same basic information: John is nervous, John looks around, John sees the clock on the wall, and John knows the time is 4:00.

Deciding which way to convey that information is a matter of emphasis. What is most important to distinguish: the character, the object, or the situation?

- As an *instruction*, it incorporates the clock and John as aspects of the *same situation.*
- As a *slug line*, it emphasizes the visual importance of the *object* (the clock).
- As a *point-of-view*, the writing prioritizes the *character* (John) as he sees the clock.

CUTAWAY

The CUTAWAY allows the screenwriter to briefly break away from a scene without creating a new scene.

- The cutaway is a short but significant departure from the *primary scene* (derived from the scene line) to an image from a *secondary scene.*

  There can be only one primary scene. Although the usual practice is to have only one secondary scene, there can be more than one.

- The cutaway must be very *brief*, so as not to detract from the continuity of the primary scene.

- The cutaway always takes place at the same time as the primary scene.

Common Applications

A cutaway is used to depict simultaneous events.

- This could be as simple as a conversation occurring in one room (the primary scene) with a concealed listener in another room (the secondary scene).

  A cutaway from the conversation to the listener, for example, could be used to create suspense, to inform the audience about what the listener overhears, or simply to remind the audience that the listener is present.

- A cutaway could also be as complex as an individual rushing though a crowded city (the primary scene) while being pursued by life-threatening enemies (the secondary scene).

Although rare (and usually clumsy), a new character could be introduced in a CUTAWAY.

Advantages

According to the conventions of Part One, which restrict the view of a scene to the location defined by the scene line, you would need to construct separate scenes for each different location.

But what if you had an activity that affects the primary scene but takes place in a location beyond the parameters of the scene line?

- You could create a new (secondary) scene.

  Doing so would interrupt the primary activity of the scene with a transition and new scene line to get to the secondary activity, only to quickly return to the continuation of the primary activity in the original scene with another transition and scene line.

  In the reading, such an approach will mislead the reader. A transition typically marks the *termination* of a scene. But in the situation just described, the scene doesn't end; it is only briefly interrupted.

- Instead of writing a new scene, you could call for a CUTAWAY that would interrupt the primary scene to briefly insert the secondary scene. The slug line RETURN TO SCENE would then get back to the primary scene.

A CUTAWAY preserves the unity of the primary scene.

Formatting

Although the CUTAWAY functions in a way that is similar to a scene, it is *not* a scene; it is a slug line. Therefore:

- It follows the capping, line spacing, and margin settings of other slug lines.

- There is no setting (interior or exterior), no time (day or night), and maybe even no location.

- It consists only of an equivalent location (which is the object of the insert).

The term CUTAWAY is followed by a dash (separated by a character-space before and after) and a few words describing the activity of the cutaway.

Terminating

Since the CUTAWAY interrupts the primary scene, it requires a RETURN TO SCENE or BACK TO . . . to resume the primary scene.

```
INT.   MARY'S DINING ROOM - EVENING

Mary is carefully preparing the table setting for two.  She
is attending to the fine details of the silverware placement.

CUTAWAY - JOHN DRIVING

He is just entering the city limits.

RETURN TO SCENE

The phone RINGS.  Mary, startled, picks up the handset.

                    MARY
              (into phone; nervous)
         Hello.
              (pause; disappointed)
         I thought it might be John.  He's late.
              (pause)
         No, I'll be fine.  Thanks.

She hangs up the phone and looks at her watch.

CUTAWAY - JOHN AT FLORIST SHOP

He buys some roses.

RETURN TO SCENE

Mary lights the table candles and lowers the room's lighting.

CUTAWAY - JOHN DRIVING

Crossing an intersection, a speeding car SLAMS into John's
car.

RETURN TO SCENE

Mary stands in front of the mirror and nervously attends to a
few details of her hair.

There is a KNOCK at the door.
```

Explanation and Notes

In this example, it is important that while we see Mary preparing to greet John (the primary scene), we also see John in transit (the secondary scene).

Because our primary area of interest in this scene concentrates on Mary, it would be distracting to write separate scenes for each cutaway to John as he approaches. By doing these cutaways, the central attention remains on Mary.

Which Is the Primary Scene?

In the previous example, the scene line

```
INT.  MARY'S DINING ROOM - EVENING
```

clearly announces that Mary's preparation for John's arrival is the primary activity.

- However, if the primary activity were John in transit, the scene line would be

```
INT.  JOHN'S CAR - EVENING
```

- The secondary activity would be Mary's preparations in the dining room:

```
CUTAWAY - MARY PREPARING DINNER
```

SERIES OF SHOTS

A SERIES OF SHOTS is the screenwriter's equivalent of a generic shopping list. The intention of any series of shots is to convey *an overall impression* in which the individual shots are less important than the thematic unity of the whole.

Applications

The series of shots can be a very useful time- and space-saving device, covering such diverse situations as the following:

- establishing an environment or activity:

```
SERIES OF SHOTS - THE MAJESTY OF THE GRAND CANYON

SERIES OF SHOTS - JOHN STUDYING FOR HIS EXAM

SERIES OF SHOTS - THE FOOTBALL GAME
```

- indicating a routine:

```
SERIES OF SHOTS - A DAY IN THE OFFICE

SERIES OF SHOTS - PROCESSING A PRISONER
```

- signaling a passage of time:

```
SERIES OF SHOTS - FROM WINTER TO SPRING

SERIES OF SHOTS - COUPLE FALLING IN LOVE
```

Advantages

A SERIES OF SHOTS allows the screenwriter to condense a number of diverse but related visuals into a unified block under a single slug line. Using such a convention saves valuable space for the screenwriter and facilitates the impression for the reader.

General Formatting

The slug line SERIES OF SHOTS is followed by a dash (separated by a character-space before and after) and a brief description of the purpose of the series.

- A good way to write such a series is to list each shot in the series by successive letters (A . B . C ., etc.), each accompanied by a brief description.

   The description of each shot in the series is usually as short as a word and no longer than a sentence. If more than a sentence is required to describe the shot, then it is probably too complex for the series and you should consider making it an independent scene.

- Each shot must be thematically related to the description in the slug line that introduces the series.

- Although there is no speciific limit to the number of shots that may be included in the series, it is typical to have between three and six shots.

Restrictions

No individual shot in the series can by itself be important enough to warrant an independent scene. It is rather the *collective impression* that is important, not the individual shots themselves.

- Do not introduce a new character (other than general groups or types) in the series.

   If, however, a character has already been introduced (in the instructions), that character can appear in the series.

- There should be no dialogue between characters in the individual shots.

Placement

The SERIES OF SHOTS can be either of the following:

- a connective technique *between scenes*, which replaces the need to write each of the shots as a separate scene

- an activity included *within a scene*, which eliminates the need to write each of the shots as a separate slug line

Although both of these applications serve a similar function, each has a different formatting requirement.

Formatting a Series of Shots between Scenes

When used between scenes, a series functions as a summary, in which the individual shots listed in the series are less significant than the unity of the series.

When used as a substitute for separate scenes:

- The series begins with a slug line that substitutes for a scene line,

   SERIES OF SHOTS

   which is followed by a dash (separated by a character-space before and after) and then a brief statement of the general purpose of the series.

   SERIES OF SHOTS – CAMPUS LIFE

- The series ends with a transition.

```
John, carrying his suitcase, steps off of the bus and smiles.

                                          DISSOLVE TO:

SERIES OF SHOTS - CAMPUS LIFE

A.   Students moving luggage, stereos, refrigerators, etc.
     into dormitory rooms.

B.   A fraternity mixer with rowdy laughter, loud music,
     carefree activities.

C.   Students studying at the library at night, coffee cups
     and soda cans at hand.

D.   The athletic field with students participating in various
     sports.

E.   A classroom.  Students carrying texts and notebooks
     file into the room and take their seats.

                                          DISSOLVE TO:
```

Explanation and Notes

To give an overview, this series summarizes many of the conventional aspects of what campus life is like. Were it not for the series, each of the five settings would need to be written as a separate scene.

Formatting a Series of Shots within a Scene

Although the SERIES OF SHOTS is most often used as a transitional device to separate sequences within a screenplay, it can be useful *within* a scene.

Unlike the application of a series of shots between scenes, the use of a series within a scene is formatted as a visual slug line.

- When used within a scene, the series concludes with a RETURN TO SCENE. When the series is finished, you can continue describing the activity of the scene.

- However, if the series ends the scene, then a transition is required (just as it would be for the end of any scene).

```
INT.  MARY'S STUDIO APARTMENT - DAY

Mary, dressed in a robe and drowsy-eyed, stumbles out of bed.
She maneuvers her way into the kitchen area.
```

```
SERIES OF SHOTS - MARY MAKING BREAKFAST

A.   Preparing the coffee maker to brew a pot.

B.   Turning on the radio and ROCK MUSIC is heard.

C.   Reading the newspaper.

RETURN TO SCENE

The phone RINGS and Mary answers it.
```

Explanation and Notes

The series can occur wherever appropriate within the scene. It can begin the scene, end the scene, or be placed anywhere in between.

A VARIATION:

Instead of RETURN TO SCENE, you could use END SERIES.

Dialogue within a Series of Shots

It is often effective to present a SERIES OF SHOTS during which dialogue is spoken. This takes the form of a *voice-over* (V.O.) that is heard while the series is being displayed on the screen.

Dialogue occurring while a series proceeds takes three forms: (1) narrator-dialogue that is not specific to any particular shot, (2) narrator-dialogue that is specifically keyed to particular shots, and (3) character-dialogue for individual shots.

- If the narrator-dialogue is spread over the series and does not correspond to any specific shots, then the complete dialogue is usually placed just after the slug line and before the series is described.

```
SERIES OF SHOTS - REFUGEES FLEEING WARSAW
                    NARRATOR (V.O.)
          Time is now short.  People are forced
          to make last-minute decisions: what
          to take, what to leave behind.  In the
          streets, a steady stream of humanity
          moves toward the main exits from the city.

A.   People in their homes, hurriedly packing small suitcases.

B.   Priceless antiques that will have to be left behind.

C.   People in twos and threes walking quickly in the night
     streets.
```

- If, however, the narrator-dialogue is associated with specific shots in the series, then the dialogue is placed just before the corresponding shot.

```
SERIES OF SHOTS - REFUGEES FLEEING WARSAW

A.  People in their homes, hurriedly packing small suitcases.

                    NARRATOR (V.O.)
           Time is now short.  People are forced
           to make last-minute decisions: what
           to take, what to leave behind.

B.  Priceless antiques that will have to be left behind.

                  NARRATOR (V.O.) (cont'd)
            In the streets, a steady stream of humanity
           moves toward the main exits from the city.

C.  People in twos and threes walking quickly in the night
    streets.
```

- Although unusual, there may be occasions when a character speaks during a specific shot in the series. Because a character is now speaking on screen, the dialogue is not a voice-over.

```
SERIES OF SHOTS - REACTIONS FROM CITIZENS

A.  John faces the camera.

                    JOHN
           It was a terrible injustice.

B.  Bill faces the camera.

                    BILL
           He didn't deserve the death penalty.

C.  Marla faces the camera.
```

WARNING:

Any character-dialogue within a SERIES OF SHOTS should be brief.

INSERTS

An *insert* is a specific shot that is (or can be) filmed at a different location and time than the scene and literally inserted into the film in post-production.

An INSERT refers to an image that

- contains pertinent information to the narrative

- occurs between scenes to link them together

- visually fills the entire screen

The image in an insert can be an *object* (such as a clock or poster) or an animated *graphic* (such as a map or diagram). An insert NEVER includes live characters.

Common Applications

Inserts traditionally have been used by filmmakers as a shorthand method of compressing long time periods or great distances. Inserts have been used to define such effects as these:

- rapidly flipping calendar pages or the spinning hands of a clock to indicate passing time
- issues of newspapers, each with a different headline flashing onto the screen, to indicate the progression of an event
- a map with the route traced in a bold line to indicate travel
- cartoon figures performing an action as a novelty

Formatting

Although an insert functions in a way that is similar to a scene, it is *not* a scene; it is a slug line. Therefore:

- It follows the capping, line spacing, and margin settings of other slug lines.
- There is no setting (interior or exterior) and no time (day or night).
- It consists only of the equivalent to a location (which is the object of the insert).

The term INSERT is followed by a dash (separated by a character-space before and after) and then the object of the insert. The INSERT slug line is usually followed by an instruction that explains or describes the purpose or activity of the insert.

Terminating

When the insert is finished, you ALWAYS end with a transition.

```
EXT.  SAN FRANCISCO AIRPORT - DAY

John's plane takes off into the sunrise.


INSERT - MAP OF UNITED STATES

An animated line starts at San Francisco then moves to Denver,
Chicago, Cleveland and ends at New York.


EXT.  KENNEDY AIRPORT - DAY
```

Explanation and Notes

In this example, the inserted map fills the screen. It is neither part of the previous scene (leaving San Francisco) nor part of the following scene (arriving in New York). It is inserted between the scenes to show the path of John's travel.

Dialogue within an Insert

Since all we see in the insert is the image (with no live characters), any dialogue accompanying the insert would be a voice-over (V.O.).

```
A plane takes off from San Francisco and disappears into the
sunset.


INSERT - MAP OF UNITED STATES

                    JOHN (V.O.)
          Okay, let's review this one more
          time.  We know he started from the
          bay area and intends to make stops
          in Denver, Chicago and Cleveland.
          In four days he'll arrive in New
          York.

As he speaks, an animated line starts at San Francisco then
moves to Denver, Chicago, Cleveland and ends at New York.


EXT.   KENNEDY AIRPORT - DAY
```

Explanation and Notes

Although there is no hard rule about where the voice-over dialogue should go in the insert, it is typically placed at the beginning and it is assumed that the dialogue is heard while the image appears.

SUBDIVIDING A SCENE INTO TWO OR MORE ACTIVITIES

Suppose you need to track two or more activities that are taking place within the same scene but occurring independently of each other.

To accomplish this, you will need to *subdivide* the scene into separate locations. Slug lines are used to establish the various subdivisions.

For example, within the scene line of

```
INT.  GRAND CENTRAL STATION - DAY
```

• You could use slug lines to partition specific areas of activity:

```
WAITING AREA
```

```
TICKET COUNTER
```

• Or you could call for views of characters who are present within the scene line:

```
JIM
```

```
TOM AND BRENDA
```

INT.   GRAND CENTRAL STATION - DAY

The huge room is CROWDED with people. Some are waiting on benches, others moving to and from trains, still others at ticket lines.

TWO DETECTIVES -

walk into the station, cautious and obviously looking for someone.

TOM AND BRENDA IN WAITING AREA

Their luggage at their side, they sit and wait impatiently.

                    TOM
          This is silly. We'd be there by now
          if we'd taken the plane.

                    BRENDA
          It's just to pacify Mother.
                    (begging for understanding)
          Please, Tom, don't start this trip
          by . . .

TICKET COUNTER

Jim, wearing dark glasses, is second in line. He seems very anxious, constantly looking around.

BACK TO DETECTIVES -

who spot Jim at the ticket counter and head toward him.

BACK TO JIM -

who sees the detectives approach but is not sure they've seen him.

BACK TO TOM AND BRENDA -

who collect their luggage and begin to walk to their gate.

THE DETECTIVES -

approach Jim, their GUNS drawn.

JIM -

quickly pulls out his GUN. He FIRES at the detectives.

THE DETECTIVES -

return FIRE.

```
THE WAITING AREA

The crowd panics as the gunshots ECHO throughout the huge
room.

BACK TO TOM AND BRENDA

They're both on the ground.  Brenda, barely conscious
with blood streaming from a shoulder wound, has
collapsed into Tom's arms.

                                               CUT TO:
```

Explanation and Notes

This example subdivides the scene (GRAND CENTRAL STATION) into three distinct fields of activity: (1) the TWO DETECTIVES searching the general area, (2) TOM AND BRENDA in the waiting area, and (3) JIM at the ticket counter.

SUBDIVIDING A MULTI-ROOM STRUCTURE INTO SPECIFIC ROOMS

Often, a narrative sequence calls for an activity that moves from room to room within a multi-room environment without any significant breaks. Rather than stopping the activity with a new scene line and transition each time the activity changes rooms, slug lines can be used to maintain the narrative flow.

As spectators, we are more likely to consider the entire structure as the scene, rather than reducing the activity to separate scenes each time the room changes.

Although used less often, this form of subdivision could refer to an outside area in which various specific locations could be analogous to the closed spaces of rooms.

Advantages

Using slug lines to control the activity maintains the unity of the scene.

Imagine the scene just described if each room were required to be a separate scene, each with its own scene line and transition. It would not read as the action would be experienced.

Formatting

The scene line would define the general structure, such as

```
INT.   ZORN'S HOUSE - NIGHT

INT.   REAL ESTATE OFFICE - DAY

INT.   COUNTY JAIL - DAY

EXT.   BALL PARK - DAY
```

The slug lines, then, would follow the characters as they moved between the various rooms.

Terminating

In the case of subdividing a multi-room structure, there would be no RETURN TO SCENE because no master shot could cover the entire structure.

```
INT.  ZORN'S HOUSE - NIGHT

The Christmas candy and cookie fest is in full swing.  The
entire house has been decorated, from the ten-foot tree to
ribbons and bows that hang from the ceiling.  GUESTS are
circulating from room to room.

THE KITCHEN

Zorn is standing at the stove, involved in removing the
steamed pudding from its mold.  A half-dozen PARTY GUESTS
are milling about, drinking and engaged in conversation.

                    ZORN
          All right, everybody.  Ready to
          go here.

He lifts the plate of pudding into the air and ceremoniously
moves into -

THE LIVING ROOM -

where a dozen MORE GUESTS are seated as they talk and drink.
Zorn places the pudding on the coffee table as the door bell
RINGS.

Anne rises from the seat in front of the fireplace and
wanders into -

THE BILLIARD ROOM -

where a small group is watching Andrew and Richard shoot a
game of Nine Ball.

BACK TO LIVING ROOM

Zorn is introducing the new arrivals to a couple next to the
tree.
```

Slug Lines within the Rooms

Each of the slug lines in this example defines a certain room in the house. Within each room, however, other slug lines could be used. For example:

```
He lifts the plate of pudding into the air and ceremoniously
moves into -

THE LIVING ROOM -

where a dozen MORE GUESTS are seated as they talk and drink.
Zorn places the pudding on the coffee table as the door bell
RINGS.

ANNE -

rises from the seat in front of the fireplace and wanders
into -

THE BILLIARDS ROOM -

where a small group is watching Andrew and Richard shoot a
game of Nine Ball.
```

WARNING:

Too much mixing of room slug lines with character/object slug lines can become confusing to follow and difficult to read.

Non-Visual Slug Lines

IDENTIFYING A CRITICAL SOUND

A sound that is critical for the dramatic tension of a scene can be expressed as a slug line.

- Although sounds are usually capped in the instructions, a sound that is critical for the dramatic tension may be more effectively written as a slug line.

- This is a matter of emphasis. The decision is based on how much the sound impacts the scene.

Formatting

As a non-visual slug line, a critical sound does not affect the view of the scene.

- A slug line that identifies a sound usually consists of a word or phrase.

- Depending on the intention, the slug line might be the source of the sound:

  THE RADIO

- Or the slug line might be an approximation of the sound itself:

  KA-CHING

  as the sound of an old-time cash register

  BONG

  as an example of a clock tower or church bell announcing the hour.

The instructions would continue in the regular manner to describe the effects of the sound.

Terminating

Because a sound is non-visual, no termination is required.

```
The couple walk the deserted street.

A GUNSHOT

They stop.  Confused, they look around.

ANOTHER GUNSHOT

Scared, they quickly duck into an alley.

ANOTHER GUNSHOT
```

Explanation and Notes

In this example, the source of the sound (GUNSHOT) is cited. As the couple walk, their attention (and ours) is interrupted by the sound of the gunshots. The reaction of the couple follows the sound of the gunshots.

```
The couple walk the deserted street.

BONG

They stop and look up.

BONG

The clock in the tower reads three.

BONG
```

Explanation and Notes

In this example, the actual sound of the clock (BONG) is imitated. As the couple walk, their attention (and ours) is interrupted by the sound of the clock as it registers the hour.

Sounds as Slug Lines or Instructions

As demonstrated in Part One, sound cues can be integrated into the instructions. Each of the preceding two examples, for instance, could have had the sounds written as instructions.

```
The couple walk the deserted street.  A GUNSHOT.  They stop.
Confused, they look around.  Another GUNSHOT.  Scared, they
quickly duck into an alley.  And a third GUNSHOT.
```

> The couple walk the deserted street. A loud BONG! They stop
> and look up. Another loud BONG! The clock in the tower shows
> three. Again, BONG!

A JUDGMENT CALL

This is one of many instances in which the screenwriter must make a decision about emphasis. How important is the sound to the scene?

- By placing the sounds as slug lines, you are making them stand out.
- Although integrating the sounds into the instructions saves space on the page, it has less impact.

In either case, the sound cues are notable. What level of prominence you assign them should reflect their influence on the scene.

EMPHASIZING SOMETHING DRAMATIC

In a movie, there will likely be events that are intended to startle the viewer. In a screenplay, a slug line can serve that purpose for the reader.

Common Applications

Because this type of slug line announces a dramatic event that should surprise the audience, you should use it sparingly. Save such a slug line for those rare moments of ultimate tension.

Formatting

Unlike visual slug lines, which re-define the master shot, dramatic slug lines do not affect the view of the scene.

- A dramatic slug line usually consists of a single word or phrase:

  SUDDENLY

  OUT OF NOWHERE

- The instructions would continue in the regular manner to describe the effects of the slug line.

Terminating

Because a dramatic slug line does not interrupt the visual component of the scene, there is no need to provide a RETURN TO SCENE.

> Matthew crosses to the counter where he pours a glass of red
> wine, swirls it and holds it up to the light.
>
> SUDDENLY -
>
> the window is SHATTERED and the wine glass EXPLODES in his
> hand.

Explanation and Notes

In this example, three words are capped. The peaceful activity of Matthew enjoying his glass of wine is SUDDENLY changed as the window is SHATTERED and the wine glass EXPLODES.

- SUDDENLY is a slug line that announces a radical change, making us jump in our theater seats.

- SHATTERED and EXPLODED are incorporated into the instructions to describe what has changed.

These events are so surprising and gripping that each is capped to emphasize its dramatic impact.

INDICATING A LAPSE OF TIME

At times, you will want to use a slug line within a scene to eliminate a period of time when nothing dramatic is happening.

Time-lapse slug lines inform the reader that the location has not changed but that some time has elapsed:

```
LATER

LATER THAT EVENING

A FEW HOURS LATER

AFTER DINNER
```

Terminating

Since a time-lapse slug line is a non-visual slug line, it does not require any form of termination. You simply write the slug line and continue with instruction or dialogue.

```
EXT.  FLORIDA CITY FISHING JETTY - EARLY MORNING

A gentle rain is falling.  The old skiff is slowly bobbing up
and down as the rain creates a pattern of ripples on the calm
water.

Haleran, his face dripping in sweat, is sitting in the skiff.
He is obviously very ill.  In an effort to rise, he slips
and falls backward, lapsing into unconsciousness.

LATER

The rain has stopped and the sun is sparkling on the still
water.

Haleran rolls to his side and tries to sit upright.
```

Explanation and Notes

In this example, the exact amount of time that has passed while Haleran has been unconscious is not important. The slug line LATER informs the reader that enough time has lapsed for the rain to have stopped and for Haleran to have regained consciousness.

PART THREE

Special Format Situations

The last one I wrote was about cattle rustlers. Before they were through with it, the whole thing played on a torpedo boat.

From the screenplay *Sunset Boulevard* (1950)
By Billy Wilder,
Charles Brackett, and
D. M. Marshman, Jr.

Note: This was the original wording from the screenplay. It was changed for the film.

This part will explain and illustrate a number of common narrative situations that require special formatting.

Parallel Action

In movie terminology, the term *action* is not restricted to car chases, karate fights, or shootouts. *Action* is any activity that happens in the scene recorded by the camera.

Parallel action is a filmmaking term that refers to sequences that are constructed around two or more actions. The viewer's attention moves back and forth between them.

Intercutting (also called *cross-cutting*) is the process of editing the actions together so as to produce a narrative connection between them. That connection, depending on the context, can serve a variety of purposes:

- chases and shootouts, in which the tension is accelerated by editing back-and-forth between pursuer and pursued or warring antagonists

- a race against time, in which characters must be at a certain location or finish a task while the clock ticks away the passing time

- the introduction of characters by intercutting episodes of their lives before they meet

Not all instances of parallel action must have an *immediate* consequence. But at some point in the narrative, their connection needs to be revealed and understood.

Common Applications

Most often, parallel action appears as sequences within a film. Variations include the following:

- Events occur at the same time in different locations. Think of:

   The helpless girl tied to the railroad tracks (first action), the hero riding to her rescue (second action), and the train approaching the helpless girl (third action)
   Suspense is intensified by intercutting.

   A view of a man's feet walking (first action) countered by a view of a woman's feet walking (second action) and culminating in the meeting of the man and woman
   The two actions imply a common destiny.

   Well-dressed, antebellum plantation owners entertaining at an opulent dinner (first action) while slaves eat paltry rations in their shack (second action)
   One action makes a comment on the other.

- Events occur at different times in either the same or different locations. Think of:

   A woman reads a letter (first action) and imagines the events described in the letter (second action).
   By intercutting, the focus is distributed between the two actions.

   An angst-ridden man passes by a location (first action) that releases the repressed memory of a traumatic situation (second action).
   By intercutting, the tension between past and present is magnified.

Less common are entire films built around a parallel action.

- For example, in Act One, a man and woman meet and get acquainted, but something happens to separate them. Act Two follows each of them as they exist in their separate circumstances. In Act Three, they find each other again and reunite.

- A few films are structured around the lives of two or more characters who are presented as essentially having separate stories. Their lives will inevitably intersect at some point, usually toward the ending.

NOTE:

Although these examples are restricted to two actions, parallel action situations can include any number of actions.

Formatting

Depending on the length and complexity of the actions, a parallel action could be written using one of three basic conventions:

- by treating the actions as separate scenes, using scene lines and transitions to move between actions
- by treating the actions as a single unified event using slug lines
- by treating the actions as a single unified event using the instructions

FORMATTED AS SEPARATE SCENES

```
INT.  ADOBE HOUSE, LIVING ROOM - DAY

Man #2 picks a semi-automatic rifle off of the wall rack and
moves to the window next to the door.


EXT.  ADOBE HOUSE, WRECKED CARS - CONTINUOUS

Wolf has made it to the wrecked cars just as Man #2 unleashes
a BURST OF FIRE from the window.

Wolf falls into the dirt as the bullets tear through the
rusted metal of the car.  He is showered with dirt and rust.


INT.  ADOBE HOUSE, LIVING ROOM - CONTINUOUS

Man #2 FIRES again and again.  Panicked, he retreats into the
adjoining kitchen area.


EXT.  ADOBE HOUSE, SIDE WALL - CONTINUOUS

Nelson looks through the window.  He can't get a clear shot
so he turns and moves along the wall to the side door.

In a practiced motion, he kicks the door open and FIRES three
shots in rapid succession.
```

```
INT.  ADOBE HOUSE, KITCHEN - CONTINUOUS

Man #2 collapses.

                                              CUT TO:
```

Explanation and Notes

In this example, what happens in each scene has been choreographed so that each action is expressed as its own scene.

The detached and disjointed nature of writing such a tightly connected instance of parallel action as separate scenes slows the reading and usually implies a slower pacing of the events.

- By dividing the actions into separate scenes, the situations are more developed.

  Generally, each action could stand as an independent story but is intercut to suggest the inevitable merger of the events.

- The introduction of multiple characters is often done in this fashion, allowing us to meet them in their own environments and circumstances before their lives intersect.

FORMATTED AS SLUG LINES

```
INT./EXT.  ADOBE HOUSE - DAY

INSIDE - THE LIVING ROOM

MAN #2 picks a semi-automatic rifle off the wall rack and
moves to the window next to the door.

OUTSIDE - THE WRECKED CARS

Wolf has made it to the wrecked cars just as Man #2 unleashes
a BURST OF FIRE from the window.

Wolf falls into the dirt as the bullets tear through the
rusted metal of the car.  He is showered with dirt and rust.

INSIDE - THE LIVING ROOM

Man #2 FIRES again and again.  Panicked, he retreats into the
adjoining kitchen area.

OUTSIDE - THE SIDE WALL

Nelson looks through the window.  He can't get a clear shot,
so he turns and moves along the wall to the side door.
```

In a practiced motion, he kicks the door open and FIRES three
shots in rapid succession.

INSIDE - THE KITCHEN

Man #2 collapses.

CUT TO:

Explanation and Notes

In this version, the slug lines provide more unity and a clearer interaction of the shootout
than in the first version.

- Using slug lines requires that all the activities fall under a single scene line (often an
  expanded scene line).

- Now the pace quickens. It's important to keep the activities contained and to treat
  them more as a *single activity* (with two or more components), than as separate
  activities.

Physical action sequences (wild car chases and super-charged shootouts) typically use
slug lines instead of scene lines to simulate the high adrenaline level the film would
assume.

FORMATTED AS INSTRUCTONS

INT./EXT.   ADOBE HOUSE - DAY

In the living room, Man #2 picks a semi-automatic rifle off
of the wall rack and moves to the window next to the door.

Wolf makes it to the wrecked cars just as Man #2 unleashes
a BURST OF FIRE from the window. Wolf falls into the dirt as
the bullets tear through the rusted metal of the car. He is
showered with dirt and rust.

Back in the living room, Man #2 FIRES again and again.
Panicked, he retreats into the adjoining kitchen area.

At the side wall, Nelson looks through the window. He can't
get a clear shot so he turns and moves along the wall to the
side door. In a practiced motion, he kicks the door open and
FIRES three shots in rapid succession.

In the kitchen, Man #2 collapses.

CUT TO:

Explanation and Notes

This version of the same action is treated as description, omitting both the individual scene lines of the first version and the slug lines of the second version.

- This approach tightly integrates the action into the descriptive passages, allowing a more flexible situation for the director.

- A potential downside of this treatment is that you, the screenwriter, are giving complete visual and pacing control of the encounter to the director.

  Instructions can be used to describe the various activities without specifying, either by scene lines or slug lines, the need to focus on any particular character or event at any particular moment.

Telephone Conversations

The term *telephone* is used here to cover any variety of sound communication devices—mobile radios, walkie-talkies, and the like.

There are three common situations for a phone conversation:

- only one participant is seen and heard

- only one participant is seen but both are heard

- both participants are seen and heard

Each of the following situations illustrates how a phone conversation might be scripted, depending on how much visual and sound information you want to give to the viewer.

FIRST SITUATION: ONLY ONE SIDE OF THE CONVERSATION IS SEEN AND HEARD

```
INT.  SAM'S TAVERN - NIGHT

Ginger is sitting at a table.  The noisy patrons are
shooting pool and playing pinball.

Ginger motions to the WAITER who produces a house
telephone from behind a counter, placing it in front of her.

She picks up the phone and punches in the numbers.

                    GINGER
               (into phone)
          Is Jerry there?
               (pause)
          Jerry, it's me.  Who was that?
               (pause)
          Oh.  I've been cooling my heels
          here for over an hour.
                    (MORE)
```

```
                    GINGER (CONT'D)
               (pause)
          Okay.  Half an hour then.
```

Ginger hangs up the phone.

Explanation and Notes

This approach is used when it is *not* important to hear what the person on the other end of the conversation is saying; our attention should be focused on the character we are seeing and hearing.

TWO VARIATIONS:

- Instead of (pause), you could use (listening), which is more specific to the on-screen activity.

- An ellipsis (...) could substitute for (pause), which would keep the conversation together in paragraph form.

```
                    GINGER
               (into phone)
          Is Jerry there? . . . Jerry, it's me.
          Who was that? . . . Oh. I've been
          cooling my heels here for over an
          hour. . . . Okay. Half an hour then.
```

Each of these two variations of writing a telephone conversation has an advantage:

- Using (pause) or (listening) more closely resembles the form of an actual telephone conversation, emphasizing the time for the response.

- Using an ellipsis saves page lines, reducing the conversation from nine lines in the first to four in the second.

However, once you begin using one convention, you should continue to use it. Flipping between the two is annoying for the reader.

SECOND SITUATION: ONLY ONE SIDE OF THE CONVERSATION IS SEEN BUT BOTH SIDES ARE HEARD

```
INT.  SAM'S TAVERN - NIGHT

Ginger is sitting at a table.  The noisy patrons are
shooting pool and playing pinball.

Ginger motions to the WAITER who produces a house
telephone from behind a counter, placing it in front of her.
She punches in the numbers.

                    WOMAN (V.O.)
               (over phone)
          Hello?
```

```
                    GINGER
               (into phone)
     Is Jerry there?

                    JERRY (V.O.)
               (over phone)
     Hello?

                    GINGER
               (into phone)
     Jerry, it's me.  Who was that?

                    JERRY (V.O.)
               (over phone)
     Landlady's here for the rent.

                    GINGER
               (into phone)
     Oh.  I've been cooling my heels
     here for over an hour.

                    JERRY (V.O.)
               (over phone)
     She was supposed to be here an
     hour ago.  Do you still want me
     to come over?
               (pause)
     It'll be at least half an hour.

                    GINGER
               (into phone)
     Okay.  Half an hour then.

Ginger hangs up the phone.
```

Explanation and Notes

In this situation, the visual focus remains on one character, but we hear both participants as they speak. Such a situation has a variety of uses:

- when it's important to keep the visuals on the first person to observe a reaction
- when you want to conceal the identity of the second person
- when you want to conceal the activities taking place on the other end of the phone

In this example, the focus remains on Ginger, the on-screen character. But it is also important to hear what Jerry, the person on the other end of the conversation, is saying.

A VARIATION:

Instead of (over phone), you could use (filtered). These are different terms but have the same meaning.

```
                    WOMAN (V.O.)
               (filtered)
     Hello?
```

```
                    GINGER
              (into phone)
        Is Jerry there?
```

Remember, once you start using a convention, you need to continue with it.

THIRD SITUATION: BOTH SIDES OF THE CONVERSATION ARE SEEN AND HEARD

In this type of situation, there are three basic ways to move between the two participants in their separate locations:

- using separate scenes to move between the participants
- using an expanded scene line and slug lines to move between participants
- by intercutting to move between participants

FORMATTED AS SEPARATE SCENES

```
INT.   SAM'S TAVERN - NIGHT

Ginger is sitting at a table.  The noisy patrons are
shooting pool and playing pinball.

Ginger motions to the WAITER who produces a house
telephone from behind a counter, placing it in front of her.

She picks up the phone and punches in the numbers.


INT.   JERRY'S BEDROOM - CONTINUOUS

The phone RINGS.  A scantily-clad WOMAN, lying on the bed,
reaches over and picks up the receiver.

Jerry, wrapped in a bath towel, comes in from the bathroom.

                    WOMAN
              (into phone)
        Hello?


INT.   SAM'S TAVERN - CONTINUOUS

                    GINGER
              (into phone)
        Is Jerry there?


INT.   JERRY'S BEDROOM - CONTINUOUS

The Woman smiles and hands the phone to Jerry.

                    JERRY
              (into phone)
        Hello?
```

```
INT.   SAM'S TAVERN - CONTINUOUS

                    GINGER
          Jerry, it's me.  Who was that?


INT.   JERRY'S BEDROOM - CONTINUOUS

                    JERRY
               (into phone)
          Landlady's here for the rent.

The Woman giggles, then starts to get playful.


INT.   SAM'S TAVERN - CONTINUOUS

                    GINGER
               (into phone)
          Oh.  I've been cooling my heels
          here for over an hour.


INT.   JERRY'S BEDROOM - CONTINUOUS

                    JERRY
               (into phone)
          She was supposed to be here an
          an hour ago.  Do you still want
          me to come over?

The Woman tugs on Jerry's towel.

                    JERRY (cont'd)
               (into phone)
          It'll be at least half an hour.


INT.   SAM'S TAVERN - CONTINUOUS

                    GINGER
               (into phone)
          Okay.  Half an hour then.

Ginger hangs up the phone.
```

Explanation and Notes

In this version, it is important to know what is happening on Jerry's end of the conversation. He is obviously lying. In such a case, the writer needs to control where the scenes cuts back and forth.

FORMATTED AS AN EXPANDED SCENE LINE AND SLUG LINES

```
INT.   SAM'S TAVERN/JERRY'S BEDROOM - NIGHT

SAM'S TAVERN

Ginger is sitting at a table.  The noisy patrons are
shooting pool and playing pinball.

Ginger motions to the WAITER who produces a house
telephone from behind a counter, placing it in front of her.

She picks up the phone and punches in the numbers.

JERRY'S BEDROOM

The phone RINGS.  A scantily-clad WOMAN, lying on the bed,
reaches over and picks up the receiver.

Jerry, wrapped in a bath towel, comes in from the bathroom.

                    WOMAN
               (into phone)
          Hello?

SAM'S TAVERN

                    GINGER
               (into phone)
          Is Jerry there?

JERRY'S BEDROOM

The Woman smiles and hands the phone to Jerry.

                    JERRY
               (into phone)
          Hello?

SAM'S TAVERN

                    GINGER
          Jerry, it's me.  Who was that?

JERRY'S BEDROOM

                    JERRY
               (into phone)
          Landlady's here for the rent.

The Woman giggles, then starts to get playful.
```

```
SAM'S TAVERN

                    GINGER
                (into phone)
        Oh.  I've been cooling my heels
        here for over an hour.

JERRY'S BEDROOM

                    JERRY
                (into phone)
        She was supposed to be here an
        an hour ago.  Do you still want
        me to come over?

The Woman tugs at Jerry's towel.

                    JERRY (cont'd)
                (into phone)
        It'll be at least half an hour.

SAM'S TAVERN

                    GINGER
                (into phone)
        Okay.  Half an hour then.

Ginger hangs up the phone.
```

Explanation and Notes

In this version, the exchange between Jerry and Ginger is kept together under the single expanded scene line. By using slug lines to move between them, the writer can exercise control over which character is on screen at any particular time.

- This allows the writer to retain the visual control because activities (beyond the phone conversation) in the separate locations are important to the scene.

- Even though it is clear that all the dialogue is through the phone, you need to keep repeating the parenthetical (into phone) because there could be side comments.

For example, one of the visuals could be expanded:

```
The Woman tugs at Jerry's towel.  Jerry struggles to keep
his composure.

                    JERRY (cont'd)
                (cupping the speaker; whispering
                to the Woman)
        Give me a moment.
                (into phone; looking at the Woman)
        It'll be at least half an hour.
```

FORMATTED BY INTERCUTTING BETWEEN PARTICIPANTS

INT.   SAM'S TAVERN - NIGHT

Ginger is sitting at a table. The noisy patrons are
shooting pool and playing pinball.

Ginger motions to the WAITER who produces a house
telephone from behind a counter, placing it in front of her.

She picks up the phone and punches in the numbers.

INT.   JERRY'S BEDROOM - CONTINUOUS

The phone RINGS. A scantily-clad WOMAN, lying on the bed,
reaches over and picks up the receiver.

Jerry, wrapped in a bath towel, comes in from the bathroom.

                    WOMAN
              (into phone)
          Hello?

INTERCUT AS NEEDED - GINGER AND JERRY ON PHONE

                    GINGER
          Is Jerry there?

                    JERRY
          Hello?

                    GINGER
          Jerry, it's me. Who was that?

                    JERRY
          Landlady's here for the rent.

                    GINGER
          Oh. I've been cooling my heels
          here for over an hour.

                    JERRY
          She was supposed to be here an
          an hour ago. Do you still want
          me to come over? It'll be at
          least half an hour.

                    GINGER
          Okay. Half an hour then.

Ginger hangs up the phone.

Explanation and Notes

In this version, it is important to hear both sides of the conversation. However, once both locations are established, it is not important which character is on screen at any given time, and the subsequent visuals are left to the director.

When using INTERCUT AS NEEDED, you can only write the conversation between the participants. You cannot describe anything visual (except as a parenthetical) because you are giving the director the control to make such decisions.

- The instruction GINGER AND JERRY ON PHONE added to the slug line INTERCUT AS NEEDED eliminates the need to repeat the parenthetical (into phone) each time the character speaks into the phone.

   However, this presumes that no side comments are included. All the dialogue is the conversation spoken on the phone.

- While in the INTERCUT AS NEEDED, there is no (V.O.) or (pause) because you are not specifying who is seen or heard at any particular time.

Car Scenes

Generally, when a scene takes place inside a stationary car, the vehicle is treated like an interior set. This suggests the following:

- The activity inside the car is more important than the activity outside the car.
- Whatever is happening outside the car is usually managed through a character's P.O.V. or is visible through the car's windows.

   For example:

```
FADE IN:

INT.  SURVEILLANCE VAN - NIGHT

Two undercover agents, GEORGE SWIFT and EDGAR PHILLIPS, are
watching through binoculars.

AGENT'S P.O.V. THROUGH BINOCULARS

At the back of a parked van, a well-dressed YOUNG MAN and a
pretty YOUNG WOMAN seem to be in the process of buying
something.  From just inside the back of the van, barely
visible, is the DEALER.

                    SWIFT (O.S.)
          I can't make the guy.  You got a fix
          on him?


                    PHILLIPS (O.S.)
          I told the Captain we'd need the night
          vision equipment for this job.
```

```
EXT.   BUILDING ACROSS THE STREET - CONTINUOUS

A car drives by and turns into an alley, playing its
headlamps across the doorway.
```

Often, when a scene takes place outside a stationary car, the car becomes the object of interest. For example:

```
EXT.   DESERTED PARKING LOT - NIGHT

The large parking lot is empty except for one car parked
almost in the middle.

A second car enters the lot from the far entrance.  It cruises
around the lot before stopping next to the first car.

The driver's door of the first car opens and RICK JONES slowly
gets out.  He is in his middle forties, dressed in Levis and a
leather jacket.  He walks around to the second car.

ANTONIO PEREZ steps out of the driver's side of the second car.
Perez is in his middle thirties wearing a suit and tie.

The two men shake hands.

                    PEREZ
          Have you got it?

                    JAMES
          In the trunk.

James opens the trunk of the first car to reveal a large
birthday cake.
```

Explanation and Notes

- Although this section focuses on cars, you could easily substitute other vehicles, such as bicycles, chariots, covered wagons, and so on. With minor adjustments, boats, trains, and airplanes can be handled in a similar manner.

- Regardless of the type of vehicle, what you must keep in mind is how much is visible in the master shot.

  If your master shot is inside a car, you will usually be able to see the outside environment through the windows. However, if you are inside an airplane, you might not be able to see what is outside.

  Similarly, if the master shot is outside the vehicle, you must consider how much of the inside will be visible.

FIRST SITUATION: **BOTH THE CAR AND LOCATION ARE IMPORTANT**

Does describing the location warrant its own scene? Should the activity in the car include glimpses of the location? Or should that decision be left to the director?

This situation can be written in one of three ways:

- as separate scenes

- as a single scene

- using an extended scene line

FORMATTED AS SEPARATE SCENES

```
EXT.  L.A. BARRIO STREET - DAY

It is raining.  Clusters of scruffy STREET PEOPLE are
huddled under storefront awnings and in sheltered doorways.

Moving slowly along the street is a beat-up CORVETTE.  There
are so many areas in "bondo" and primer that the original
red color is hard to find.


INT.  CORVETTE - DAY (MOVING)

John is driving, Harry is in the passenger seat.

                    HARRY
          You don't think it's too early?  I
          mean, I'd like to think you got me
          over here because something was going
          to happen.

                    JOHN
              (pointing out the window)
          Enough action for you?

HARRY'S P.O.V. - OUT THE WINDOW

On the corner, TWO MEN are manhandling a large CRATE marked
"U.S. Government Property" into a van.

                    HARRY (O.S.)
          What can I say?  When you're right,
          you're right.
```

Explanation and Notes

- This example gives a clear sense of the barrio and introduces the beat-up Corvette on the street before we enter the car with John and Harry.

- For the scene inside the Corvette, (MOVING) alerts the reader that the car is being driven, in this case, through the barrio.

FORMATTED AS A SINGLE SCENE

```
INT.  CORVETTE - DAY (MOVING)

John is slowly driving through a L.A. barrio.  Harry is in
the passenger seat looking out the window.  It is raining.

Outside, clusters of scruffy STREET PEOPLE are huddled under
storefront awnings in sheltered doorways.

                    HARRY
          You don't think it's too early?  I
          mean, I'd like to think you got me
          over here because something was going
          to happen.

                    JOHN
               (pointing out the window)
          Enough action for you?

HARRY'S P.O.V. - OUT THE WINDOW

On the corner, TWO MEN are manhandling a large CRATE marked
"U.S. Government Property" into a van.

                    HARRY (O.S.)
          What can I say?  When you're right,
          you're right.
```

Explanation and Notes

The second version keeps all the activity inside the car. From within the car, we can see the barrio, but because it is now background, it is given less importance.

What the writer saves is an exterior scene that serves to establish the location. What the writer loses is the emphasis on the barrio and the description of the beat-up Corvette.

FORMATTED AS AN EXTENDED SCENE LINE

```
EXT./INT.  L.A. BARRIO STREET/CORVETTE - DAY

L.A. BARRIO STREET

It is raining.  Clusters of scruffy STREET PEOPLE are
huddled under storefront awnings and in sheltered doorways.
```

Moving slowly along the street is a beat-up CORVETTE. There are so many areas in "bondo" and primer that the original red color is hard to find.

CORVETTE (MOVING)

John is driving, Harry is in the passenger seat.

> HARRY
> You don't think it's too early? I mean, I'd like to think you got me over here because something was going to happen.

> JOHN
> (pointing out the window)
> Enough action for you?

HARRY'S P.O.V. - OUT THE WINDOW

On the corner, TWO MEN are manhandling a large CRATE marked "U.S. Government Property" into a van.

> HARRY (O.S.)
> What can I say? When you're right, you're right.

Explanation and Notes

The third variation uses an expanded scene line to give the impression that the barrio and the Corvette are closely linked. This is preferable if there is significant interaction between what's happening on the street and what's happening inside the car.

The expanded scene line ties the two locations together and allows the director to make the visual choices.

SECOND SITUATION: TWO OR MORE CARS ARE ENGAGED IN A CHASE

The high-speed momentum and sense of unexpected danger that accompany a car chase regularly provide some of the most exciting sequences in motion pictures.

Car chases will typically be written in one of two ways:

- as instructions

- with slug lines

FORMATTED AS INSTRUCTIONS

FADE IN:

EXT. CITY STREETS - NIGHT

A PORSCHE is racing through the streets, changing lanes, darting in and out of traffic. Other motorists brake and swerve to avoid being hit. A POLICE CAR chases the Porsche through the crowded streets until the police car crashes.

Explanation and Notes

This brief description leaves to the director a variety of choices: How many near misses? How many close calls? Are people hurt?

FORMATTED AS SLUG LINES

FADE IN:

EXT. CITY STREETS - NIGHT

A flurry of activity. Theaters are letting out, outdoor cafes are busy, late night stores are open, cars crowd the streets.

SUDDENLY -

a PORSCHE squeals down the exit ramp of a parking garage and spins onto the street. It quickly accelerates down the street.

MOVING WITH THE PORSCHE -

as it careens into a parked car, forcing it up onto the busy sidewalk as PEDESTRIANS scramble out of the way.

Without hesitating, the Porsche speeds up and moves back into its lane as it speeds by -

A POLICE CAR PARKED AT A CURB

Seeing the Porsche, the police car starts its engine and takes off in pursuit.

MOVING WITH THE PORSCHE -

as it comes up on a CROWDED INTERSECTION with cars stopped at a red light. It swerves onto the sidewalk, taking out a news stand and several parking meters. Terrified PEDESTRIANS are jumping out of the way.

The Porsche veers off the sidewalk through the intersection and back into the correct lane. Three other cars in cross traffic COLLIDE when first one hits the brakes.

THE POLICE CAR -

follows along the sidewalk. It too exits the sidewalk but SLAMS into the three-car pile-up in front.

THE PORSCHE -

continues down the street, around the corner and out of sight.

THE POLICE CAR

TWO OFFICERS stagger out of the car, bewildered. They stare at the destruction in disbelief.

Explanation and Notes

In this version, the car chase is choreographed in much more detail. In exercising such control over the description, the writer has provided a graphic sense of the chase.

THIRD SITUATION: ACTIVITY OCCURS BOTH INSIDE AND OUTSIDE A CAR

It is quite common to have scenes in which action occurs both inside and outside a car. An expanded scene line can incorporate both activities.

EXT. MIAMI BEACH STREET - DAWN

The Mercedes is driving too fast. It passes a parked truck and speeds through a stop sign.

INT. MERCEDES - CONTINUOUS (MOVING)

Arnie looks to his right. Too late. He spots an idling POLICE CRUISER.

                ARNIE
      Oh, man!

The blare of a POLICE SIREN and he looks in -

THE REAR VIEW MIRROR -

where the FLASHING LIGHTS of the cruiser are close behind.

RETURN TO SCENE

Arnie pulls the car over and waits.

EXT./INT.   MERCEDES - CONTINUOUS

The cruiser has stopped behind the Mercedes. The door opens,
a POLICE OFFICER gets out and walks to the car.

Arnie rolls down the window and fumbles through his wallet as
the Officer reaches the driver's side of the car.

The Officer looks in the window.

                    OFFICER
          In a hurry this morning, are we?
          License and registration, please.

Arnie hands over the documents.

                    ARNIE
          I know I was going too fast, but I
          really didn't see the stop sign with
          that truck parked there.

                    OFFICER
          I don't think you could see me, either.

                    ARNIE
          I was up all night . . . at the office . . .
          and . . .

                    OFFICER
          Been doing some drinking?

                    ARNIE
          No, just exhausted. I caught a few
          hours sleep with . . . and I'm on my way
          home to my wife and daughter.

The Officer hands the documents back to Arnie.

                    OFFICER
          Go home to your wife and daughter.
          But if I ever catch you speeding again,
          I'm going to read you your rights.

As the officer walks back to his cruiser, Arnie breathes a
sigh of relief.

FOURTH SITUATION: A CAR PASSES BY A FIXED POSITION

```
FADE IN:

EXT.   DESERT HIGHWAY - DAY

The countryside is still and silent.  Distant mountains
surround the flat desert area.

LOOKING DOWN THE ROAD

A small SPECK in the far distance.  The faint rumble of a big
block ENGINE.

As the speck approaches, it is recognized as a green MUSTANG
going flat out.  The engine sound intensifies as the car
races closer.  In an instant, the Mustang speeds by and
continues up the road.

LOOKING UP THE ROAD

The Mustang passes into the distance and the engine sound
fades.
```

Explanation and Notes

In this variation, our viewing position is fixed. Since the "speck" is not identified at the beginning, it could be almost anything. As it comes closer, we identify it as a car. And then, still in our fixed view, we watch as it speeds by and disappears into the distance.

Televised and Projected Images

Televised and projected images appear on a regular basis in contemporary films.

Televised images can include

- a television set
- a surveillance or security monitor
- a studio monitor
- a video conference call

Projected images can include

- a film projected in a movie theater
- a slide or computer presentation (such as PowerPoint)

How such a televised or projected source is formatted depends on its prominence in the scene. There are two basic situations:

- The image is seen within the *master shot.*

  In this situation, the televised or projected image is one element in the scene. It may have something to do with the narrative, or it may be just part of the background.

- The image is isolated by a *slug line.*

  In this situation, the master shot is interrupted by a slug line that accentuates the televised or projected image. The image, therefore, becomes the center of our viewing interest.

FIRST SITUATION: **TELEVISED IMAGES**

FORMATTED AS PART OF THE MASTER SHOT

```
INT.  TURNER'S LIVING ROOM - EARLY EVENING

Michael is attentively watching the television while sitting
comfortably on the couch.

On the television, the LOGO for "Eye-Witness Evening Report"
appears over a news set.  THREE ANCHOR people are in place as
the THEME MUSIC plays.

                    ANNOUNCER (V.O.)
                 (on television)
          Welcome to the six o'clock Eye-Witness
          Evening Report with Glenn Stevens and
          Sally Evans, featuring Vince Styles with
          the sports and Holden Faust with the
          weather.  And now, Sally Evans.

                    MICHAEL
                 (calling to the kitchen)
          Hey, Jill, Sally's doing the news tonight.

The television displays SALLY EVANS, middle thirties,
pertly efficient.  Michael sits up, interested.

                    SALLY
                 (on television)
          Good evening.  Two masked men held up
          the Southwest branch of Home Federal
          Savings and Loan early this afternoon.

Jill appears through the kitchen doorway and looks at the
television.
```

```
                    SALLY (cont'd)
                  (on television)
        But the would-be thieves, having locked
        their keys in the getaway car, were forced
        to abandon their loot and flee the scene
        on foot as the police arrived.

                    JILL
        She looks good.
                  (to Michael)
        Dinner'll be ready in ten minutes.
```

Explanation and Notes

In this example, Michael and Jill as well as the television personalities are equally part of the scene, with the dialogue alternating between the couple in their apartment and the newscasters on television.

Keeping everything within the master shot leaves decisions about moving between the couple in the living room and the newscasters on television up to the director.

Television as Background

In the preceding example, if Michael and Jill were engaged in an important conversation with the television playing in the background, then they would need to be kept in the position of prominence.

- When describing the scene, you could write

  ```
  The TELEVISION plays in the background.
  ```

  and leave decisions about what program is playing to the director.

- If a type of program (a specific show or a particular movie) is required, then you need to clearly describe that. You could simply write

  ```
  In the background, the LOCAL NEWS plays on the television.
  ```

By capping TELEVISION, you indicate that what is on the television is not important; it is only important that the television is on. By capping LOCAL NEWS, you are indicating that the kind of program is important but the specific content is not.

FORMATTED AS SLUG LINES

```
INT.  SPORTS BAR - NIGHT

The group at the bar is totally absorbed by the BOXING MATCH
that is playing on the television mounted on the wall behind
the bar.  CHEERS and BOOS from the barroom spectators
alternate as the action proceeds.

THE TELEVISION SCREEN - A BOXING MATCH

The BELL rings and the boxers come out battling.  It is an
exciting match as the contestants trade punches.
```

The pace of the match is fast, hard blows being exchanged by each of the boxers.

                    RINGSIDE COMMENTATOR (O.S.)
                 (over television; excited)
             This match has more than lived up to
             the hype.

Suddenly, one of the boxers is knocked to the canvas and the referee begins the count.

                    BARROOM SPECTATOR (O.S.)
             This is the fight of the year!

THE BAR

The group ROARS with excitement.

Explanation and Notes

The slug line (THE TELEVISION SCREEN — A BOXING MATCH) draws our viewing attention to the boxing match that everyone is watching.

While we are looking at the televised images, we hear two instances of off-screen dialogue:

- While we're watching the boxers on television, the Ringside Commentator is not seen. His commentary, therefore, is (O.S.).

  However, were the Commentator to appear on the televised image, then he would *not* be (O.S.). He would be treated as a regular character.

- Also (O.S.) is the comment from the Barroom Spectator, who we cannot see while we're looking at the television.

SECOND SITUATION: PROJECTED IMAGES

FORMATTED AS PART OF THE MASTER SHOT

INT. CONFERENCE ROOM - DAY

The large room is set up like a make-shift theatre. Various PLAIN CLOTHES and UNIFORMED officers are seated facing a screen in the front of the room.

Into the room walk Evans and JASON WILKES, mid-thirties in a clean-cut suit. They stand in front of the screen.

                    EVANS
                 (to the group)
             This is CIA Deputy Director Jason
             Wilkes. He will be conducting this
             briefing.
                 (to the back of the room)
             Lights, please.

The room goes dark. On the screen, a SLIDE PROJECTOR throws the image of a BEARDED MAN.

> WILKES
> This is Christian Van Horne, one of the
> most vicious assassins on the current
> list. We have reason to believe that
> he is here to kill Senator Hawkins.
> > (to the back)
> Next slide, please.

The image changes to another slide with Van Horne and three OTHERS.

> WILKES (cont'd)
> Here he is in Amsterdam last August with
> three members of his team. The one on
> the left is Jessica Aviner, the other two
> are the Jensen brothers.
> > (to the back)
> Next slide.

Explanation and Notes

In this example, the projected images reveal what the assassins look like. One advantage of a slide or movie presentation is that the room is dark so the viewer is forced to look at (and remember) the images.

FORMATTED AS SLUG LINES

INT.   MOVIE THEATRE

John and Mary Ellen are working their way down the dark aisle looking for seats.

THE MOVIE SCREEN - THE MOVIE BEGINS

A driveway with a Brough Superior motorcycle toward the lower left of the screen. From the right side, Peter O'Toole walks across the screen carrying a fuel can. The MUSIC intensifies as the title "Lawrence of Arabia" appears.

JOHN AND MARY ELLEN IN THEIR SEATS

> JOHN
> (whispering; passionate)
> Do you know how long I've waited for this
> restoration? I hope they found the
> goggles scene.

```
Mary Ellen glances at him with an insincere smile, clearly
bored.

                           MARY ELLEN
               How long did you say this lasts?

BACK TO THE MOVIE SCREEN

Lawrence is on the motorcycle speeding down a winding
country road.
```

Explanation and Notes

In this example, slug lines are used to move between John and Mary Ellen as they sit in the theatre and the movie as it plays on the screen.

Time-Shifts and Flashbacks

A conventional screenplay narrative moves through a chronological progression of events, from a beginning to a conclusion. Sometimes, for dramatic effect, that chronology may need to be broken as the narrative travels back into the past or leaps ahead into the future to reveal relevant details.

There are two basic ways for a narrative to *jump* to a different time:

- through a forward or backward **time-shift** in the narrative
- through a character's **flashback** of a previous event or situation

What is the difference between the two chronological breaks?

- A time-shift takes the *entire narrative* to a different period in the story.
- A flashback is specific to *one character's perception* of the past.

FIRST SITUATION: TIME-SHIFTS

When we speak of a *time-shift* in a screenplay, we are referring to a major break in the chronology.

- Any backward movement in the narrative is a time-shift.
- But when the narrative is moving forward, a time-shift represents a *major* narrative leap.

NOTE:

A progression from one scene to the next that merely eliminates a relatively small amount of time (usually a few hours, a day or two, or even a week or month) is usually not regarded as a time-shift. The term represents a *significant* jump in time, often allowing for speculation about what has happened during the interval.

In general, there are two ways to indicate a time-shift:

- The scene line can be used to include a parenthesis that specifies the jump in time.

- A superimposed text can be used to announce the jump to the audience.

When a time-shift occurs, you only include that information the first time you make the time-shift.

WARNING:

Because a time-shift breaks the normal flow of the story, you must be very careful not to create unintended confusion.

FORMATTED AS PART OF THE SCENE LINE

```
                    MR. JOHNSON
                 (stiffly)
          I'll pick you up in four years when you
          graduate.

                    RALPH
          A snap.  See you in four.

Mr. Johnson mechanically shakes Ralph's hand, then returns to
the car and drives off.

                                            FADE OUT:


FADE IN:

INT.  LARGE COMMENCEMENT AUDITORIUM - DAY (TEN YEARS LATER)

At the podium, Ralph, decked out in cap-and-gown, is in line
with other expectant UNDERGRADUATES to receive his diploma.
```

Explanation and Notes

When you use a scene line to include information about the narrative jumping between the present and either the past or the future, the reader will assume that you are always in the time-shift you specify until you specify something different.

- In the preceding example, if the narrative proceeds to follow Ralph after graduation without making any additional radical leaps into the future, then no further information needs to be included (in parentheses) in subsequent scene lines.

- If, however, further into the story, the narrative takes Ralph back to his college years, then you must include that information (in parentheses) in the appropriate scene lines.

Indicating a specific time-shift in the scene line only informs the *reader*. How to clarify the shift in time to the *audience* must be written either in the instructions or left to the director.

FORMATTED AS A SUPER IN/OUT

```
Mr. Johnson mechanically shakes Ralph's hand, then returns to
the car and drives off.

                                                   FADE OUT:


FADE IN:

INT.  LARGE COMMENCEMENT AUDITORIUM - DAY

SUPER IN/OUT - "TEN YEARS LATER"

At the podium, Ralph, decked out in cap-and-gown, is in line
with other expectant UNDERGRADUATES to receive his diploma.
```

Explanation and Notes

Using a superimposed message directly informs the audience about the time-shift.

SECOND SITUATION: FLASHBACKS

Using flashbacks is the most common way for the screenwriter to delve into the past of a character. Because flashbacks represent a character's subjective account of the past, they frequently serve to explain that character's motivations.

- Most often, flashbacks are the *visual memory* of a character.

  What we are seeing on-screen is taken by the audience to be the character's literal and truthful recollection.

  In some instances, however, we later discover the flashbacks to be falsified (as in a lie), biased (perhaps incomplete), or mistaken (as in self-deception).

- Flashbacks can also take the form of *visualized testimony.*

  For example, suppose a witness in a courtroom provides an account of an event. What we see on screen is a visualized reconstruction of the witness's verbal testimony, which may be accurate, misinterpreted, or even totally false.

  Visualized testimony can also take the form of a character reading a letter and imagining the content of the letter as he or she reads it.

Regardless of whether the flashback is based on a character's memory or imagination, it is formatted in the same manner in a screenplay.

Since flashbacks typically function to reveal information that is otherwise unknown, they must be carefully planned. Keep these considerations in mind:

- The narrative must clearly identify whose flashback we are about to enter and when the flashback is finished.

- The narrative must clearly return us to that character.

- There is no limit to the number of characters who may have flashbacks, and there is no limit to the number of flashbacks a given character can have.

Flashbacks can function in three fundamental ways:

- as a complete scene (or a series of complete scenes)
- as part of a scene
- as progressive fragments

When a flashback is introduced with a slug line, it must end with a terminating slug line. There are three options for doing so.

The first two—END FLASHBACK and RETURN TO SCENE—take us back to the master shot of the scene.

The third option is to use a slug line to take us to the character in the scene, for example:

    BACK TO GLENN

When the flashback is the complete scene, then you must end it with a transition.

ABOUT THE EXAMPLES

The screenplay used in the next several examples follows an award-winning photojournalist (Glenn) who received a commendation for an evocative Vietnam War photograph. But Glenn has kept a secret for many years: He took this photograph at the expense of an unconscionable act.

Glenn has successfully repressed the circumstances surrounding the photograph for many years, but something happens that begins to re-awaken the unsavory memory. Although there have been dialogue references to his coverage of the Vietnam War, this is the first visualization of his experience in the war.

FORMATTED AS A COMPLETE SCENE

```
INT.  GLENN'S APARTMENT - DAY

Glenn moves to the chess board, takes the BLACK KNIGHT from
the board and clasps it tightly in his hand.  He stares at the
piece, deeply, as though he shares some special secret with
the Knight.

                                              DISSOLVE TO:


EXT.  VIETNAM RICE PADDY - DAY (FLASHBACK)

As seen through a CAMERA VIEWFINDER, a SOLDIER is playfully
posing for the camera with a chess piece, a BLACK KNIGHT
raised in victory.


                    SOLDIER
              (to the camera; jubilant)
         After all these years, I finally beat you!

SUDDENLY, from nowhere, a VIET CONG jumps the soldier from
behind.
```

The camera's MOTOR DRIVE clicks off several images as the Viet Cong has one arm around the soldier's throat while his free hand is wielding a commando knife.

The soldier is terrified.

> SOLDIER (cont'd)
> (to the camera; screaming)
> For God's sake, get him off me. Kill him!
> Kill him!!!!

The camera's MOTOR DRIVE continues as the Viet Cong repeatedly stabs the soldier.

The camera follows the soldier as he slips to the ground.

The bloodied hand of the soldier, twitching in the last moments of life, clutches the black Knight. The MOTOR DRIVE takes a few more images.

Rapid GUN FIRE kills the Viet Cong.

> DISSOLVE TO:

INT. GLENN'S APARTMENT - DAY (BACK TO PRESENT)

Glenn angrily throws the Knight against the far wall. But he can't throw it far enough to outreach the memory.

> CUT TO:

Explanation and Notes

The (FLASHBACK) in the scene line immediately alerts the reader that this is *not* another scene in the linear narration but an interruption that gives us background material. By using the (FLASHBACK) instruction, the screenwriter is informing the director that the audience should know that this scene is a flashback.

- Flashbacks that appear as complete scenes are often introduced by a DISSOLVE or FADE.

- If a flashback warrants its own scene, then it is introduced with a scene line, the same way any scene is introduced.

  The only difference in format between the flashback as a complete scene and any regular scene in the narrative is that (FLASHBACK) is added to the scene line. Otherwise, the scene follows the same format as any other scene.

- If the flashback continues for more than one scene, then it is not necessary to include (FLASHBACK) in each scene line after the first; it is assumed that we are still in the flashback until the script cues us that the time is again the present.

- When the narrative returns to the present, then (BACK TO PRESENT) should be added to the end of the new scene line.

FORMATTED AS A SLUG LINE WITHIN A SINGLE SCENE

```
INT.   GLENN'S APARTMENT - DAY

Glenn moves to the chess board, takes the BLACK KNIGHT from
the board and clasps it tightly in his hand. He stares at the
piece, deeply, as though he shares some special secret with
the Knight.

VIETNAM RICE PADDY (FLASHBACK)

As seen through a CAMERA VIEWFINDER, a SOLDIER is playfully
posing for the camera with a chess piece, a BLACK KNIGHT
raised in victory.

                         SOLDIER
                (to the camera; jubilant)
            After all these years, I finally beat you!

SUDDENLY, from nowhere, a VIET CONG jumps the soldier from
behind.

RETURN TO SCENE

Glenn angrily throws the Knight against the far wall.  But he
can't throw it far enough to outreach the memory.

                                                   CUT TO:
```

Explanation and Notes

This is the same scenario as the previous one, except that this time, the memory of Glenn's Vietnam experience is presented as a brief interruption of the scene.

Using this technique, the flashback is formatted as a slug line. The only difference in format between a flashback and a typical slug line in a scene is the addition of (FLASHBACK) at the end. The RETURN TO SCENE ends the flashback and resumes the scene with Glenn in his apartment.

A VARIATION

Instead of the (FLASHBACK)/RETURN TO SCENE in the previous example, the same effect could be written using a BEGIN FLASHBACK/END FLASHBACK format.

```
BEGIN FLASHBACK - VIETNAM RICE PADDY

As seen through a CAMERA VIEWFINDER, a SOLDIER is
playfully posing for the camera with a chess piece, a
BLACK KNIGHT raised in victory.

                     SOLDIER
                (to the camera; jubilant)
          After all these years, I finally beat you!
```

           SUDDENLY, from nowhere, a VIETCONG jumps the soldier from
                behind.

           END FLASHBACK

FORMATTED AS A SERIES OF SLUG LINES WITHIN A SINGLE SCENE

INT.   GLENN'S APARTMENT - DAY

Glenn moves to the chess board, takes the BLACK KNIGHT from
the board and clasps it tightly in his hand. He stares at the
piece, deeply, as though he shares some special secret with
the Knight.

VIETNAM RICE PADDY (FLASHBACK)

As seen through a CAMERA VIEWFINDER, a SOLDIER is playfully
posing for the camera with a chess piece, a BLACK KNIGHT
raised in victory.

                     SOLDIER
              (to the camera; jubilant)
        After all these years, I finally beat you!

SUDDENLY, from nowhere, a VIET CONG jumps the soldier from
behind.

RETURN TO SCENE

Glenn moves to a cupboard where he removes a bottle of Scotch
and pours a hefty amount into a tumbler.

VIETNAM RICE PADDY (FLASHBACK)

The camera's MOTOR DRIVE clicks off several images as the
Viet Cong has one arm around the soldier's throat while his
free hand is wielding a commando knife.

The soldier is terrified.

                 SOLDIER (cont'd)
             (to the camera; screaming)
        For God's sake, get him off me. Kill him!
        Kill him!!!!

RETURN TO SCENE

Glenn downs the Scotch in one hefty swig.

VIETNAM RICE PADDY (FLASHBACK)

The camera's MOTOR DRIVE continues as the Viet Cong repeatedly
stabs the soldier.

```
The camera follows the soldier as he slips to the ground.

The bloodied hand of the soldier, twitching in the last
moments of life, clutches the black Knight.  The MOTOR DRIVE
takes a few more images.

Rapid GUN FIRE kills the Viet Cong.

RETURN TO SCENE

Glenn angrily throws the Knight against the far wall.  But he
can't throw it far enough to outreach the memory.

                                                    CUT TO:
```

Explanation and Notes

When the complete flashback is broken into fragments, it is called a *progressive flashback.* This device is often used when, for example, unpleasant memories are forcing their way back into a character's conscious mind.

NOTE:

Progressive flashbacks are usually fashioned as interruptions, either within a single scene or spread over a series of scenes.

- The flashback fragments are usually brief at first but get progressively longer as the memory pushes itself forward.

- Each flashback adds a layer to the initial fragment of memory, until the incident can be completely understood.

Unusual Scene Beginnings

Scenes normally begin with a scene line and open with the master shot describing the characters on screen and what they're doing. But occasionally, you will want to begin a scene in a different way.

There are three basic situations that differ from the traditional master shot:

- a scene that begins with a *sound* before the image appears

- a scene that begins with a *text* before the image appears

- a scene that opens with a *visual slug line,* rather than the master shot

FIRST SITUATION: A SCENE THAT BEGINS WITH SOUND BEFORE THE IMAGE APPEARS

Suppose that it will be helpful to your narrative for a sound to be heard before any image appears on the screen.

Such a sound could include someone answering a telephone, a police siren, an alarm clock, or the like.

```
FADE IN:

The sensual beat of JAZZ MUSIC begins and grows louder.


EXT.  DESERT CAMPSITE - NIGHT

The MUSIC continues and seems distinctly out of place against
the bleakness of the terrain.

With only the moonlight for illumination, the figure of a
YOUNG MAN carrying a GHETTO-BLASTER appears.
```

Explanation and Notes

In this example, the spectator imagines a visual accompaniment associated with the jazz music (perhaps a wild party or a jazz club). As the image of the isolated and foreboding desert campsite appears, it seems a sharp contrast to the music.

A WARNING:

Such a contrast can't be done just for the effect. The spectator will feel cheated if it has no "pay-off." What is the point of the contrast?

SECOND SITUATION: A SCENE THAT BEGINS WITH TEXT BEFORE THE IMAGE APPEARS

Some narratives require that certain information (background or introductory) be given in advance of a scene to the spectator. One way to do this is with a text message to the audience.

```
FADE IN:

TEXT OVER BLACK SCREEN

        The year is 2050 and the world has survived
        a devastating global war that has destroyed
        over ninety percent of the world's population.
        Numerous bands of renegade militia are
        competing for power in the new world order.


EXT.  A PASTORAL COUNTRYSIDE - DAY

Into a peaceful meadow ride a dozen horse-mounted MILITIA.
```

THIRD SITUATION: A SCENE THAT BEGINS WITH A VISUAL SLUG LINE BEFORE THE MASTER SHOT

This situation occurs when the first image of a scene focuses on a specific person or object, thus preventing us from identifying the physical location (the master shot), as specified in the scene line.

```
INT.  SECURITY OFFICE - DAY

SURVEILLANCE VIDEO

Approaching the main entrance of the building is a GRUNGY MAN,
dressed in a sweatshirt and jeans.  The image freezes and
zooms in to get a close-up view of the man's face.  Although
the image is a bit fuzzy, the features of the man's face can
be seen.

THE SECURITY OFFICE

Dwayne looks at the frozen image on the monitor.  He presses
a button on a video unit and a copy of the image on the
monitor screen rolls out of the printer.
```

Explanation and Notes

In this example, the scene does not open the way most scenes open. Rather than beginning with a view of the security office (the master shot), this scene opens with the image on a surveillance video (a visual slug line).

- Whether we see only the video or some of the security office or the monitor console is the director's decision. The slug line SURVEILLANCE VIDEO indicates that the video is what dominates the screen.

- Once the image freezes, the view of the entire security office is available as Dwayne makes a print-out of the video image,

Unusual Effects

Unusual effects generally fall into one of three categories:

- special effects
- strange creatures
- strange environments

How *detailed* the effect needs to be depends on several factors:

- If it is the big event of the narrative, then you will probably want to give it a fairly graphic description.

- If, however, there are a number of such circumstances, then perhaps you will need to limit your description.

- You may elect to only allude to the effect and to leave the particulars to the production team.

As the writer, you should not be concerned about how expensive an effect might be or how difficult it might be to realize on screen. Write the effect the way you imagine it, and let the production team figure out how to make it happen.

FIRST SITUATION: SPECIAL EFFECTS

In a screenplay, you don't use the term *special effects* or its acronym, *SFX*. Instead, you just describe the effect in the instructions.

FORMATTED AS A DETAILED DESCRIPTION

Amanda steps out of the jeep and cautiously approaches the precious artifact. As she nears, the crystal begins to GLOW. She stops in her tracks, puzzled.

SUDDENLY, the sky begins to cloud over. The WIND intensifies as DIRT PARTICLES begin to swirl around the dig site.

Amanda looks upward as small rocks begin to TUMBLE down from the cliff above her.

The ground begins to TREMBLE and larger rocks now cascade down the cliff onto the dig site. Amanda tosses the sketch on the ground as she reaches for the crystal, the prize about to be won.

The crystal's glow spills over into a white-hot ENERGY FIELD which focuses into separate beams of light that spread out to form a perfect square. The entire area is encompassed.

The sky explodes with ominous claps of THUNDER and flashes of LIGHTNING.

Fearful, Amanda gives up and races back toward the jeep. The falling rocks cascade down the cliff blocking the jeep's path.

With a terrifying ROAR, the mountain tumbles down.

EVERYTHING in the gully--Amanda, the jeep, the crystal--is buried under tons of stone.

Clouds of dust and debris billow upward, consuming the entire area.

THE SKY ABOVE

The dark clouds begin to clear as an EAGLE soars overhead.

                                                    DISSOLVE TO:

This incident could have been written with a less detailed description, allowing the specifics to be interpreted by the production team.

FORMATTED AS A MINIMAL DESCRIPTION

```
Amanda steps out of the jeep and cautiously approaches the
precious artifact.  As she nears, the crystal begins to GLOW.
She stops in her tracks, puzzled.

A SPECTACULAR DISPLAY -

of magical lights and energy fields as the entire area is
engulfed.  The mountain tumbles down, burying both the
crystal and Amanda.

                                                DISSOLVE TO:
```

SECOND SITUATION: STRANGE CREATURES

Strange creatures can include aliens, cyborgs, mutant or altered humans, or mythological or supernatural deities—in short, anything not regarded as normal.

As when describing special effects, you use the instructions to describe the look and behavior of a creature.

In a screenplay, a strange creature, like a human character, requires an introduction. This means you cap the creature's character-name and provide an appropriate description.

```
INT.  TECH LAB - DAY

Johnson and Andrews are hovering over the egg-shaped capsule,
which is resting on a lab table in a make-shift cradle.

Overhead is a series of pull-down power tools.  Andrews
reaches up and pulls down a hand-held laser device.  He
switches it on, tests its range, makes an adjustment, and
begins to carefully cut around the circumference of the
capsule.

As Andrews completes his cut, Johnson activates a hand-control
suction device and lifts off the top of the capsule.

Inside are the remains of a small CREATURE.  Though definitely
not human, it possesses a smooth, metallic-looking head but
without eyes, nose, or ears.  The Creature has two stumps
instead of legs but no torso or arms.

Suddenly, a section across the front of the head LIGHTS UP
from the inside.  The lit area moves from side to side, as if
the Creature is looking for something.

Andrews and Johnson stare in amazement.
```

THIRD SITUATION: **STRANGE ENVIRONMENTS**

```
INT.   SPACESHIP CORRIDOR

The long corridor consists of dozens of triangular section
modules about twelve feet long and twelve feet on a side.
The side walls are partially glazed with small square windows,
and between the windows are randomly located exit hatches.

At the junction between groups of three modules are solid
triangular DOOR PANELS, accompanied by wall-mounted control
panels.

Lt. Jackson proceeds down the corridor.  He stops at the first
door and punches a code into the control pad.  The three
triangular sections pivot at the corners and open like a
camera iris.

The operation completed, Lt. Jackson cautiously steps through
the opening into the next section.
```

Explanation and Notes

As with special effects and strange creatures, how precisely you describe a strange environment will depend on its significance.

- In this instance, a detailed description of the environment and procedure is provided by the writer because later in the screenplay, the opened door will trap someone by closing prematurely.

  Capping DOOR PANELS draws the reader's attention to the importance of the setting.

- If this activity had no particular narrative importance, it could be written quite simply:

  ```
  Lt. Jackson walks down a long high-tech looking corridor.
  He opens the door and proceeds into the next section.
  ```

  This would then leave all of the detail to the imagination of the director and set designer.

Unusual Character Introductions

Normally, a character is introduced (named and described) when he or she first appears on-screen. But from time to time, a central character will need either to appear or to speak *before* an appropriate introduction can be provided.

There are three basic situations in which a character appears but his or her introduction is delayed by:

- describing a character's environment before introducing the character
- seeing a character who enters the story before being properly named
- envisioning an imaginary character who is visible only to a real character

A character who is not present can be introduced by:

- a still image (a photograph, portrait or drawing)

- a voice

NOTE:

These introductions are typically restricted to primary characters.

FIRST SITUATION: AN ENVIRONMENT IS DESCRIBED BEFORE THE CHARACTER IS INTRODUCED

```
FADE IN:

INT.   GRAHAM SOUTHERLAND'S OFFICE - DAY

Neatly arranged in a wall display are RACING MEMORABILIA.  A
photograph of a young boy next to a soap box derby racer with
the number "31".  A silver trophy for First Place--Grand Prix
of England and numerous other racing trophies.  A PHOTOGRAPH
of a man in his late twenties with a  moustache standing
behind a Lotus Grand Prix car with the number "31".  A world
championship trophy for Formula One.  A series of photos of
sports racing and Grand Prix cars in front of a building with
a sign reading "Southerland Motors, Ltd."

At the end of the display wall, GRAHAM SOUTHERLAND, early
sixties, is asleep in a wheelchair.  He is clearly the same
man as in the photograph, although now he's old and gray.
```

Explanation and Notes

By beginning with a description of Graham Southerland's wall, which is laden with his trophies and awards as a race car driver, we know a good deal about him before we ever see him.

- When we do see him, we regard him less as an anonymous older man confined to a wheelchair than as a man who has had an exciting, dangerous, and triumphant past.

- When we learn that he is now in his sixties, interesting questions come to mind: Did a racing injury confine him to the wheelchair? Surrounded by displays of his victories, is he living in the past? Where will the story go?

SECOND SITUATION: A CHARACTER ENTERS THE STORY BEFORE BEING NAMED

```
INT.   SURVEILLANCE VAN - NIGHT

Undercover agents Swift and Tonelli are watching through the
side window as a drug deal is going down at the side of a
black van parked across the dimly lit street.
```

At the back of the parked van, a well-dressed YOUNG MAN and a pretty YOUNG WOMAN are talking to the DRUG DEALER who is barely visible.

Swift looks through the binoculars.

> SWIFT
> I told the Captain we'd need the night vision equipment.

EXT.   BUILDING ACROSS THE STREET - CONTINUOUS

Lurking in the shadows of the doorway stands a MYSTERIOUS FIGURE. There is not enough light to see more than the vague image of a man in an overcoat and fedora hat.

A car drives by and turns into an alley, passing its headlamps across the doorway. The Mysterious Figure has vanished.

EXT./INT.   SURVEILLANCE VAN - CONTINUOUS

Wearing a leather jacket and a backward Yankees cap, a YOUNG THUG is sneaking along the driver's side of the surveillance van. He is holding an automatic pistol.

When he reaches the driver's side window, the Young Thug presses the muzzle against the side of Swift's head.

> YOUNG THUG
> You ladies lookin' for somethin', or just out for a night on the town?

Swift drops his binoculars. Tonelli looks over in shock.

> YOUNG THUG (cont'd)
> Put your hands on the wheel.
> (to Tonelli)
> You, hands on the dash.

BEHIND THE YOUNG THUG -

is the Mysterious Figure with his pistol behind the Young Thug's baseball cap. He presses the barrel against the Yankees logo.

> MYSTERIOUS FIGURE
> I'm not going to count to three. Put up the piece.

The Young Thug relaxes his pistol. Swift immediately disarms him. He peers behind the Young Thug and sees the Mysterious Figure who is revealed to be CAPTAIN ANDERSON.

```
                          SWIFT
           Captain Anderson.  What are you doing here?


                          CAPTAIN ANDERSON
           Saving you idiots.
```

Explanation and Notes

For dramatic purposes, the writer has chosen not to reveal the identity of Captain Anderson when we first encounter him.

- At the beginning of the scene, introducing this character as MYSTERIOUS FIGURE shades his presence with danger. What is he doing there? Is he another drug dealer?

- As the scene progresses, we find that the Mysterious Figure is actually another police official. To reveal this earlier would have undermined the situation of danger that presents itself to the two agents.

Once Agent Swift identifies the figure as Captain Anderson, he can subsequently be referred to as CAPTAIN ANDERSON.

THIRD SITUATION: AN IMAGINARY CHARACTER APPEARS

Imaginary characters are similar to strange creatures in certain ways. The difference is typically that imaginary characters will look and function like human characters, whereas strange creatures will have a recognizably alien appearance.

As spectators in the audience, we can usually see and hear imaginary characters. However, within the world of the film, their presence and recognition is usually limited.

- Usually, at least one real character will be able to see and hear an imaginary character.

- If there are multiple imaginary characters, they will usually be able to see and hear each other.

Imaginary characters can be spirits (ghosts, demons, angels) or hallucinations (psychic creations) that assume a human appearance.

- If, in the screenplay, imaginary characters perform like normal humans (that is, if they have physical bodies that can be seen and heard by the audience), then they should be written as if they were real characters.

- As the writer, however, you must be especially careful to establish and adhere to the "rules of behavior" for any imaginary character. Who can see and hear the imaginary character? Does the imaginary character act independently of any other character, or is it dependent on the character who imagines it?

```
FADE IN:

INT.  DOCTOR'S OFFICE, WAITING ROOM - DAY

Seated is DAVID SIMMONS, mid-thirties, good looking, wearing
a jogging outfit.  Next to him on the banquette are MARTHA
EDWARDS, late twenties, looking younger in jeans and a
button-down man's shirt, and EMILY ANDERSON, slightly older,
gorgeous, also wearing a jogging suit.
```

```
                    DAVID
                (to Emily)
        So, when's Richard due back?
                (taking Martha's hand)
        We should all get together . . . maybe
        go out on the boat.  I can't wait
        for him to meet Martha.


                    MARTHA
        Oh, David, please don't make such a
        fuss.


                    EMILY
        No, no.  You should make a fuss, and
        the day on the boat sounds terrific.  I'm
        just not sure how soon.  He's been away
        for almost three weeks and I'm not that
        eager to share him right now.
```

David and Martha look at each other and laugh. They
affectionately squeeze each other's hands.

The door to the inner office opens and -

IN THE DOORWAY -

appears DR. ANDREW JACOBSEN, sixties, dressed in a lab coat.

```
                    DR. JACOBSEN
        David, come in.  I've got the results
        of those tests.
```

RETURN TO SCENE

David is sitting alone. No Martha. No Emily. David gets up.

Explanation and Notes

When the scene opens, David, Martha, and Emily are all introduced as real characters and thus seen and heard by us. There is no reason to suspect otherwise.

It is only when Dr. Jacobsen enters that we find out things are not as they seemed. Martha and Emily do not exist except in David's mind.

FOURTH SITUATION: A CHARACTER IS INTRODUCED BY A STILL IMAGE

```
INT.  DAVID FIELD'S LAW OFFICE - DAY

Field sits behind a large desk.  He is clearing off the last
of a pile of papers and handing them to Susan.
```

                              FIELD
                  The top two are for dead files. The
                  bottom one under Ramirez, pending.
                  Thanks, Susan.

Susan takes the papers and heads to the door. She stops at
the doorway to let Len Sanders into the room, then leaves.
Sanders is carrying a large expandable file.

                              SANDERS
                       (pointing to the file)
                  We've got three days. Everything you
                  need about Jameson should be in here.

Sanders hands the file to Field and waits while Field leafs
through it. Legal documents. Transcripts. An arrest report.
And a glossy PHOTOGRAPH.

                              FIELD
                  Anton Jameson. Age 47. Fleeing
                  the scene.

                              SANDERS
                  Look at the photo.

Field takes a long look at -

THE PHOTOGRAPH -

of a good-looking man, late thirties, in a jacket and tie.
At the bottom, printed in the white border, is "Anton Jameson.
Contact: The D.G. Baker Talent Agency."

RETURN TO SCENE

Explanation and Notes

According to the procedures defined in Part One, the name Anton Jameson cannot be capped when Sanders looks at his photograph, because even though Jameson will soon be a major character, he is not yet physically present.

• Since Jameson's name can't be capped, attention must be drawn to him by using the glossy photograph. PHOTOGRAPH is capped because it is the prop that alerts us to his impending importance.

• When Jameson appears in person, his name will be capped.

WARNING:

This is a rare situation. It occurs when a character is first shown in a photograph and will later have some narrative significance. It is essential for us to be able to recognize that character when he or she physically appears.

FIFTH SITUATION: A CHARACTER IS INTRODUCED BY A VOICE

On some occasions, a character may be introduced by voice. The voice can come from any of several sources:

- Most often, the voice will come from a telephone or some other mechanical device.

- It could be a voice that is first heard off screen.

- It could be a disembodied voice that comes from a spiritual source.

```
FADE IN:

INT.  DR. EMMA SMITH'S OFFICE - DAY

DR. EMMA SMITH, early forties, good looking, conservatively
dressed, is seated behind her desk reading a file.  She is
surrounded by piles of earmarked books, file folders, legal
pads that seem to crowd her out of the small office.

The intercom BUZZES.  She reaches over and presses a button.

                    DR. SMITH
               (into intercom)
          Yes, Janice?

                    RECEPTIONIST (V.O.)
               (over intercom)
          Dr. Smith, it's Richard Andrews.  He
          sounds really bad.

                    DR. SMITH
               (into intercom)
          Put him through.

She releases the intercom button, reaches for a legal pad and
a pen, then takes a deep breath as she picks up the receiver.

                    ANDREWS (V.O.)
               (over phone)
          Doc, it's happening again.  No matter
          what you say, I know I'm guilty.

The VOICE of Richard Andrews is raspy, perhaps asthmatic.

                    DR. SMITH
               (into phone)
          Richard, calm down.  You know we've
          discussed this.  There's been no report of
          a crime or anyone answering her description.
          I thought we were in agreement that . . .
```

```
                        ANDREWS (V.O.)
                 (over phone; interrupting)
         You were in agreement. I know what I've
         done.
```

Explanation and Notes

This situation is very similar to one in which a character is first presented as a still image.

Like a character first presented by an image, the name of a character first presented as a voice cannot be capped in the instructions because he or she is not physically present in the scene. When that character speaks, however, his or her name is capped as a character-name in the dialogue-block.

- In this example, Andrews warrants such attention because he is a major character and the audience needs to be able to recognize this voice as his. A subsequent scene will depend on this recognition.

- Because the receptionist is not significant to the narrative, it would be misleading to attribute qualities to her voice.

A Character's Appearance or Demeanor Changes

A character will sometimes need to change in appearance (so that we will not recognize him or her) or demeanor (so that his or her behavior will be so different as to take the form of a different character).

Such changes usually apply to the following situations:

- a character who appears at different ages
- a character who masquerades as someone from the opposite gender
- a character who is introduced in disguise but whose real identity is later revealed
- a character who has multiple identities or who is demonically possessed

FIRST SITUATION: A CHARACTER APPEARS AT DIFFERENT AGES

Typically, this variation refers to ages that are spread across a significant span of time. This frequently occurs when an adult character reflects back on a more youthful period.

- On-screen, the age differences will be visibly obvious because each phase will either be played by a different actor or by the same actor with dramatically different make-up.

- In the screenplay, however, the difference can be made clear by altering the character-names assigned to the various phases of the character's life.

The first time we are introduced to the character, a character-name will be given. At subsequent phases, the character will be re-introduced and assigned a variant of the original character-name.

```
FADE IN:

INT.  CHILD'S BEDROOM - DAY

A 12-year-old child, YOUNG DANNY HARRIS, is sitting on his
bed reading.  He has shaggy hair and wears clean blue jeans
and a tee-shirt.  One arm is in a new plaster cast.

The walls of the room contain posters from classical music
festivals, including a Pablo Casals concert.  In one corner is
a music stand, a straight-backed chair, and propped in the
corner is a CELLO.

                                              DISSOLVE TO:


INT.  CHILD'S BEDROOM - DAY (15 YEARS LATER)

This is the same bedroom as before, but the furnishings are
completely different, more modern.  The walls have water color
paintings of rural scenes hanging in a neat row.

DANNY HARRIS, now age 27, sits on the side of the bed.  He is
over six feet tall, wears faded Levis with a black sleeveless
Harley-Davidson tee-shirt.  Both arms have leather cuffs from
the wrist to almost the elbow.

The door opens and a YOUNG WOMAN in a plain house dress stands
in the doorway.

                         DANNY
          Thanks.  I just wanted to see the old
          room again.

He stands and follows the woman out the door.
```

Explanation and Notes

In this example, the main character is presented at two distinctly different ages. Since the difference is enough to significantly change his appearance, he will be treated as if he were two different characters: YOUNG DANNY as a child and DANNY as an adult.

The variants in the character's name should make it easy for the reader to distinguish the differences.

SECOND SITUATION: **THE AUDIENCE IS AWARE THE CHARACTER IS DISGUISED**

```
INT.   BASEMENT RECREATION ROOM - DAY

Jack, Tom and Willie are seated around a card table, writing
notes on legal pads.  There are piles of papers on the table,
and piles of crumpled sheets around the floor.

Jack sits back and tosses his pen on the table.

                    JACK
          I can't believe we let ourselves get
          conned into this mess.  What were we
          thinking?

                    TOM
          We were thinnking, "How hard can this
          be?  They're women."  Anyway it's way
          too late to be wondering.

                    WILLIE
          We have to find out--exactly--what
          they're up to.

                    TOM
          Forget about it.  There's no way on
          ladies' night and we've run out of time.

                    WILLIE
          Maybe we can bribe the bartender.  You
          know.  Get him to tell us.

                    JACK
          Who's gonna pay him?  You?  Certainly
          not me.  No, the only solution is to
          get one of us in there.

Tom and Willie stare at Jack, waiting for him to reveal his
brainstorm.

Jack gets up from the table and crosses to the laundry area
in the corner of the room.  He rummages through a basket of
clothes and returns to the table.

He dumps a pile of women's clothing on the table and proceeds
to hold up items of apparel for inspection.
```

```
                        JACK (cont'd)
        I guess there's an unexpected benefit to
        my divorced sister moving back in.


INT.  HARRY'S CLUB - NIGHT

The crowded club is wall-to-wall WOMEN.  The only men in are
three BARTENDERS who are flipping bottles for the customers.

Sitting at the end of the bar is Jack, dressed in his
sister's clothes.  With a wig, some make-up and bits of
padding, he appears to be a passably attractive woman.

One of the flipping bartenders approaches Jack.

                        BARTENDER
        What'll you have, young lady?

Jack turns and looks over his shoulder, then realizes he is
the one being addressed.

                        JACK (as JACKIE)
                    (in a falsetto voice)
        How are your Margaritas?

                        BARTENDER
        Best in town.  Shall I make one just
        for you?

                        JACK (as JACKIE)
        All right.

Jack scans the room, looking for the women.  He spots them at
a corner table.
```

Explanation and Notes

This example has Jack only briefly posing as a woman. If, however, Jack were to play Jackie for a lengthy period and, as the writer, you wanted the audience to begin thinking of Jack as Jackie, then you might consider using separate character-names to keep their different identities separate.

THIRD SITUATION: THE AUDIENCE IS UNAWARE THE CHARACTER IS DISGUISED

This screenwriting situation is typically used when you don't want the audience to know that a character who has already been introduced is appearing in a disguise that will purposefully lead the audience to believe that he or she is a new character. It will then be a surprise for the audience to discover who that character really is.

In such a situation, you will write the character in the disguise as a new character, and revert to the character's established name once his or her disguise has been revealed.

Colonel Smith and Special Agent James Nance walk to the door.

                    COLONEL SMITH
          I don't care what it takes. Just
          get the damned thing.

EXT.   RUSSIAN-AMERICAN CHECKPOINT AREA - THAT NIGHT

An UGLY OLD WOMAN limps toward the Russian guard station.
She is dressed in tattered dirt-covered rags and is mumbling
to herself.

She is stopped by a RUSSIAN GUARD.

                    RUSSIAN GUARD
          Papers, please.

He holds out his hand, waiting for her to pass the papers,
then catches a whiff of her stench and winces.

                    RUSSIAN GUARD (cont'd)
          God, woman, what's the matter with you?

                    UGLY OLD WOMAN
          I'm sick, you fool.

The Ugly Old Woman bends over and starts to gag. The Guard
pulls back and waves her through the gate.

The Ugly Old Woman limps across the neutral zone to the U.S.
checkpoint, stopping to cough, before reaching the U.S.
GUARD.

                    U.S. GUARD
          Hold it, ma'am, I need to see your . . .
                    (beat)
          Are you all right?

                    UGLY OLD WOMAN
                    (straightening up)
          Fit as a fiddle, Martin. Where's
          Colonel Smith? Tell him I've got "the
          damn thing."

The Ugly Old Woman strips off her rags and face make-up. She
is revealed to be Special Agent Nance.

                    AGENT NANCE
          Fooled you too, didn't I?

Explanation and Notes

In some instances, a previously identified character may appear in a disguise so that he or she will seem to be a different character. In that situation, the disguised character must be treated as a new character (with a character-name and description). When his or her real identity is revealed, then you will revert back to that character.

FOURTH SITUATION: A CHARACTER HAS MULTIPLE IDENTITIES OR PERSONALITIES

This screenwriting situation is typically used in the following instances:

- A character displays a personality disorder, such as schizophrenia.

- A character plays the role of a different character, such as an actor or a spy.

- A character is possessed by another personality, such as an alien or demon.

- A character has an established identity but can be transformed into another identity, such as a superhero.

In each case, the same actor would play both roles, even though the character-names would change.

```
INT.   POLICE INTERROGATION ROOM - DAY

Seated at a table in the middle of the small room are Dr.
Knight and Officer Henderson.  Jack Evans, wearing shackles
and a prison jumpsuit, is seated across from them.

A tape recorder on the table is running.

                    HENDERSON
          For the record, state your full name.

                    JACK
               (defiant)
          Evans.  Jack Evans, and no matter what
          you morons think, I'm in charge here.

                    HENDERSON
          Okay, Jack, you're in charge.

                    JACK
          Damn right.

                    DR. KNIGHT
          If that's so, Jack, you could arrange
          for us to talk with John.

                    JACK
          Why?  He's weak.  He can't help you.

                    HENDERSON
          We have important questions for him.
```

```
                         JACK
            I told you he's weak and he's a liar.

                       DR. KNIGHT
            Jack, if John is weak and a liar,
            why are you afraid to let him talk?

                         JACK
            Me, afraid?  I'll show you who's afraid.

Jack hangs his head for a moment.  When he looks back up, his
demeanor has significantly changed.  He is now JOHN, calm and
controlled.

                       JACK/JOHN
            Hello, Dr. Knight.  Good to see you.

                       DR. KNIGHT
            Hello, John.  Good to have you back.
```

Explanation and Notes

In this example, Evans has two distinctly different personalities, which are manifested as Jack and John.

- Since the personalities are so distinctly different, the writer has opted to emphasize the difference by referring to Evans as JACK when he is in that persona and as JACK/JOHN when he is in the alternate persona.

- In such a situation, the choice of whether or not to use different character-names is an important one. The decision rests on two significant factors: (1) How much screen-time does the character occupy? and (2) How meaningful is it for the audience to believe in the different personalities?

A VARIATION:

When Jack loses his personality to the personality of John, his character-name could be written as

```
                       JACK (as JOHN)
            Hello, Dr. Knight.  Good to see you.
```

Dreams and Fantasies

Similar to flashbacks, a character's psychic experience can be revealed through dreams and fantasies.

A dream or fantasy can be treated in either of two ways:

- clearly identified to the viewer as a dream or fantasy
- disguised as reality and later revealed to the viewer as a dream or fantasy

A unique characteristic of formatting dreams and fantasies is that, by nature, they can be less specific in location and time than traditional narrative scenes. Therefore, dreams and fantasies lend themselves to more abstract descriptions.

- A scene line for a dream or fantasy could be as vague as

  ```
  A DREAM
  ```

  or as specific as

  ```
  EXT.  THE SKY - DAY
  ```

- The screenwriter needs to convey the *mood* or *feel* of the dream or fantasy state and trust the director to render the particulars.

A dream or fantasy is formatted like a flashback. It can be any of the following:

- a complete scene (beginning with a scene line)

- inserted into a scene (introduced by a slug line)

- a progressive series of fragments

FIRST SITUATION: A DREAM OR FANTASY THAT IS CLEARLY IDENTIFIED

When you want the audience to be immediately aware that they are inside a character's mind, experiencing a dream or fantasy, you should include that information in either a scene line or a slug line.

```
A DREAM

The screen goes blinding white as we see THE SUN.  The WIND
is deafening, much too loud to be normal.

An EAGLE soars, momentarily shielding us from the light.  It
dips, picks up a thermal and soars again.

From the Eagle/Dreamer's SUBJECTIVE VIEW high above the
ground, the barren desert landscape appears minute.  The
horizon tilts slowly back and forth as the Eagle/Dreamer
soars.

The horizon suddenly disappears as the Eagle/Dreamer FREE
FALLS.

The WIND increases and blends with the Eagle's SCREECHING.

Seeming to float in space, in front of the Eagle/Dreamer, is
a CRYSTAL with smooth-faceted surfaces.

Light is gathered into the top surface of the crystal and
projected as a BEAM onto the ground far below.

The Eagle SCREECHES again, a screech that takes on a human
quality as the ground comes closer and closer.

END OF DREAM
```

Explanation and Notes

In this example, there really is no defined setting, location, or time. It is simply a dream. The spirit appears and is perceived as illusory rather than real. The description, therefore, represents the experience of the dream.

SECOND SITUATION: A DREAM OR FANTASY THAT IS DISGUISED AS REALITY

You may want to delay the identification of a dream or fantasy and treat it as though it were within the same physical realm as the narrative.

In such a situation, viewers will realize this to be a dream or fantasy only *after* it has been concluded.

```
INT.   MELISSA'S BEDROOM - NIGHT

Melissa is stretched out in her bed.  She seems comfortably
snuggled under her blanket.  Through the open window, a dog's
BARK awakens her.

She sits up in bed, anxious.  In a smooth movement, she tosses
the blanket aside, gets out of the bed, and walks over to the
window.  She hesitates a moment, then she jumps outside.

She starts her fall from the high-rise to the street below
when -

SUDDENLY -

Melissa is startled awake, sitting bolt upright in her bed.
Terrified.  Sweating.

                                              DISSOLVE TO:
```

Explanation and Notes

To make this example work, the writer must present Melissa's actions as though they are occurring in the real world and thus avoid giving away the surprise. What was perceived as Melissa's jump will then be shown to be a bad dream.

Because the surprise is the key to the incident, you don't want to reveal that Melissa's suicide is a dream. Therefore, you would *not* include A DREAM as part of either a scene line or a slug line.

Written Material On-Screen

Written or printed material usually appears in the form of a letter, newspaper article, or diary entry. If the material is to be shared with the audience, it can be formatted in one of three basic ways, depending on the specific situation:

- Viewers don't see the content of the material, but they hear a character read it aloud.

- Viewers don't see the content of the material, but they hear it through the character's mind as the character reads it.

- Viewers see the content of the material and read it for themselves.

FIRST SITUATION: THE CONTENT OF A LETTER IS READ ALOUD

A letter that is verbalized should be formatted the same as conventional dialogue. However, because the dialogue is quoting a source, the content of the letter should be enclosed in quote marks.

```
Mary passes Mina's letter to Jonathan.  He opens it and
examines the content.

                         JONATHAN
                    (reading the letter)
              "My dearest.  This is to tell you that I
              must leave this evening for Transylvania
              to become the bride of Count Dracula."

Jonathan drops the letter and looks at Mary.  There are tears
in his eyes.
```

Explanation and Notes

In this example, we do not see the content of the letter. We only hear it as Jonathan reads it aloud to Mary.

Therefore, this text should be formatted like conventional dialogue, including the parenthetical (reading the letter).

- The quotation marks indicate that the material Jonathan is reading is the content of Mina's letter.

- In the preceding example, it is clear that when Jonathan speaks, he is reading the letter. However, within the same dialogue-block, Jonathan could both read Mina's letter *and* speak to Mary. For example:

```
Mary passes Mina's letter to Jonathan.  He opens it and
examines the content.

                         JONATHAN
                    (reading the letter)
              "My dearest.  This is to tell you that I
              must leave this evening for Transylvania
              to become the bride of Count Dracula."
                        (to Mary)
              What am I going to do?

Jonathan drops the letter and looks at Mary.  There are tears
in his eyes.
```

In this situation, the quotation marks clearly separate the letter from the dialogue.

SECOND SITUATION: THE CONTENT OF A LETTER IS HEARD THROUGH THE MIND OF THE READER

In the previous example, the content of the letter that is verbalized is placed within quotation marks to indicate that another person's words are being quoted by the reader.

However, in the following example, quotation marks would *not* be used because the words belong to the speaker.

```
Mary passes Mina's letter to Jonathan.  He opens it and
examines the content.

                    MINA (V.O.)
          My dearest.  This is to tell you that I
          must leave this evening for Transylvania
          to become the bride of Count Dracula.

Jonathan drops the letter and looks at Mary.  There are tears
in his eyes.
```

Explanation and Notes

In this example, we hear Mina's voice (indicated by the V.O.) as if Jonathan is hearing her voice in his mind.

A VARIATION:

If, instead of Mina's voice, you wanted to hear Jonathan's voice as he read the letter *to himself,* then you would use JONATHAN (V.O.).

THIRD SITUATION: THE CONTENT OF A LETTER IS DISPLAYED ON-SCREEN

Unlike the preceding two examples, this form is *not* verbalized. Instead, we read the letter itself.

Because the content of the letter is similar to dialogue, it should be formatted as if it were dialogue but without a character-name attached to it.

```
Mary passes Mina's letter to Jonathan.  He opens it and begins
to silently read.

THE LETTER

          My dearest.  This is to tell you that I
          must leave this evening for Transylvania
          to become the bride of Count Dracula.

RETURN TO SCENE

Jonathan drops the letter and looks at Mary.  There are tears
in his eyes.
```

Explanation and Notes

In this example, the slug line THE LETTER indicates that we are seeing the letter on the screen. Even though the instructions are that Jonathan begins to read the letter, he does so silently.

A WARNING:

If the letter is intended to appear on screen (and not to be recited by a character), the viewer must read it. It is therefore a good idea to keep the material short.

An Emblem or a Sign

Many screenplays require that a *text* (a sign, label, etc.) or a *graphic* (a logo, emblem, symbol, etc.) be recognized by the viewer.

The usual practice is to place the content of the text or a description of the graphic in the instructions and to enclose it with quotation marks or write it in all caps. Do not, however, use both quotes and caps.

```
The man is wearing an identity badge that announces him as
"Officer Wolf, New Mexico State Police".
```

```
Parked at the curb is a truck with the LOGO of the "Teledyne
Corporation" on the door.
```

Explanation and Notes

Never place a graphic rendering (an image, drawing, diagram, etc.) of what the emblem or sign should look like in the screenplay.

However, if the look of an emblem or sign is significant, then it is appropriate to provide a written description. (But do *not* include a graphic; that is the job of the production designer.)

Stock Footage

It is occasionally necessary to use *stock footage* in a screenplay. This term usually refers to camera footage that has been previously shot and preserved in an archival library.

The most common source of stock footage comes from newsreel material, which can lend a sense of history or period to a story. When called for in a screenplay, stock footage can take either of two forms:

- authentic (actually footage shot at the time)
- simulated (created to represent the time)

For purposes of screenwriting, this distinction is usually not relevant. All stock footage—whether authentic or simulated—is treated as though it were the real thing.

```
INT. - THEATRE SEATING AREA - CONTINUOUS

The newsreel is in progress.  Haleran and Donna Jo enter the
theater and find their seats.

An episode of "The March of Time" is in progress.  The voice
of the NARRATOR resounds throughout the theater.

STOCK FOOTAGE - THE FALL OF PARIS

                    NARRATOR (V.O.)
               Hitler continues to push his Panzer
               divisions at a breakneck pace.  His
               blitzkrieg tactics have already brought
               most of Europe to its knees.

STOCK FOOTAGE - WAR PRODUCTION IN ENGLAND

                    NARRATOR (V.O.)(cont'd)
               Meanwhile, the people of England brace for
               what appears to be the inevitable.

STOCK FOOTAGE - AMERICAN DESTROYERS

                    NARRATOR (V.O.)(cont'd)
               Doing our part, the United States has
               traded 50 destroyers to the tiny
               island empire, bravely standing alone
               against Hitler's assault.
```

Foreign Languages
(with or without Sub-Titles)

```
INT.   NAVAJO HOGAN - AFTERNOON

Wolf and Chris enter the hogan and sit on the ground.  It is
dark, the only light coming from the doorway and the smoke
hole overhead.

ASTIDI SANI, aged but serene, is crouching near the center of
the room, his back to the visitors.  He is CHANTING.

                    CHRIS
               (whispering to Wolf)
               What's he doing?

Wolf stops her with a gesture to keep silent.
```

As Astidi Sani finishes his chant, he turns to his guests.

>   ASTIDI SANI
>   (in Navajo with sub-titles)
>   The Blessing Way, nephew.
>
>   WOLF
>   (in Navajo with sub-titles)
>   Yes, Uncle, I remember.
>   (acknowledging Chris)
>   I have brought a friend.
>
>   ASTIDI SANI
>   (in Navajo with sub-titles)
>   I am pleased.

Chris, confused, smiles at Astidi Sani.

>   WOLF
>   (to Chris)
>   Come closer.

Explanation and Notes

- Unless there is an instruction, it is assumed that the characters in a scene are speaking in English.

- When a character speaks in a foreign language, it must be indicated. That can be done in one of two ways:

>   ASTIDI SANI
>   (in Navajo)
>   I am pleased.

indicates that the character is speaking the words in Navajo but there are *no sub-titles*.

>   ASTIDI SANI
>   (in Navajo with sub-titles)
>   I am pleased.

indicates that he is speaking in Navajo and the sub-titles translate the words.

- It is also permissible to mix the two languages. Just be sure that the parentheticals indicate which dialogue is spoken in the foreign language and whether it is to be translated for the audience.

Title Cards

A movie will on occasion deliberately break its narrative into clearly distinguishable *episodes*, and each episode will be introduced by a *title card*. (*Title*, in this usage, does not refer to the title of the film but to the title of the episode within the film.)

- Title cards are similar to SUPERIMPOSITIONS in that they offer a text message to the audience. Whereas the text of a SUPER is imprinted on the image on the screen, the text of a TITLE CARD is printed on a plain (usually black) screen or an illustration.

- The use of title cards is a motif in the narrative. After the first title card, it is assumed that the rest of the film will include more title cards.

Title cards in film are the equivalent of chapter headings in literature. Each one begins a new section of the narrative.

A title card is written as a slug line that is inserted between scenes.

- It follows the same type look and line spacing as any other slug line.

- It appears after a transition and before the next scene line.

```
Peter walks to the door and slams it shut as he storms out.

                                                    CUT TO:


TITLE CARD - "PETER MEETS KATHLEEN"

EXT.  SHOPPING CENTER, FOOD PLAZA - DAY

Peter is walking toward the theater's ticket counter when -

                         FEMALE VOICE (O.S.)
               Peter?

Peter stops and looks around, confused.

                         FEMALE VOICE (O.S.)
               Peter.  It's me.  Kathleen.

Peter spots Kathleen, looking very attractive and vivacious,
sitting at one of the outdoor tables.  Across from her is her
MOTHER.

Peter, pleasantly surprised, walks over to their table.
```

Explanation and Notes

Inserting the title card ("PETER MEETS KATHLEEN") breaks the narrative into distinct episodes. Each subsequent episode would be introduced in the same manner.

PART FOUR

Common Format Mistakes

A writer writes from his gut, and his gut tells him what is good and what's merely adequate.

From *Barton Fink* (1991)
Screenplay by Joel and Ethan Coen

A number of formatting mistakes are both typical and frequent.

- Most are simple oversights that are easy to correct.
- For many formatting problems, there are multiple solutions.

This part is not intended to be comprehensive. Rather, it provides a limited but representative selection of mistakes that can easily undermine the credibility of an otherwise fine screenplay. Those who have the power to move a screenplay along the development path have no tolerance or patience with such mistakes.

If your screenplay is going to be rejected, let it be rejected for its content. It is inexcusable to undermine all the hard work that goes into the writing of a screenplay by making format errors, such as the ones described in this section.

General Mistakes

USING INCORRECT LINE SPACING

For certain written materials—for instance, term papers, creative manuscripts, and newsroom copy—the standard is to have additional spacing between lines of type. For a screenplay, however, this is not acceptable.

THE ORIGINAL VERSION:

```
FADE IN:

EXT.  OAK POINT FOREST, A CLEARING - DAWN

The clearing is in the middle of a stand of oak trees, bounded
on two sides by the branches of a stream.  Into this pastoral
setting walk a young couple.  JENNIFER OWENS is in her early
twenties, attractive with long blonde hair.  She is dressed in
a bright sun dress and is admiring an engagement ring.

With her is a YOUNG MAN, also in his early twenties.  They are
casually strolling.  Each has one arm firmly wrapped about the
other's waist.  The Young Man is carrying a rucksack.

                         YOUNG MAN
              This is it.  The special place.

                         JENNIFER
              You were right.  It is beautiful.
```

Use the Proper Line Spacing

Just as using an incorrect typeface will throw the page count of a screenplay off, so will using incorrect line spacing.

- A reader gauges the approximate running time of a screenplay on the basis that, on average, 1 page of screenplay translates to 1 minute of film time. A screenplay needs to be about 110 pages (give or take 10 pages) for a standard running time of between 100 and 120 minutes.

- The previous example uses 1 $\frac{1}{2}$ line spacing, which would extend the length of a conventional screenplay from 110 pages to about 150 pages.

The only acceptable line spacing for a screenplay is single spacing, with blank lines where appropriate.

A CORRECTED VERSION:

```
FADE IN:

EXT.   OAK POINT FOREST, A CLEARING - DAWN

The clearing is in the middle of a stand of oak trees, bounded
on two sides by the branches of a stream.  Into this pastoral
setting walks a young couple.  JENNIFER OWENS is in her early
twenties, attractive with long blonde hair.  She is dressed in
a bright sun dress and is admiring an engagement ring.

With her is a YOUNG MAN, also in his early twenties.  They are
casually strolling.  Each has one arm firmly wrapped about the
other's waist.  The Young Man is carrying a rucksack.

                         YOUNG MAN
               This is it.  The special place.

                         JENNIFER
               You were right.  It is beautiful.
```

USING AN INCORRECT TYPEFACE

The vast array of available typefaces makes it tempting to select a personal favorite.

THE ORIGINAL VERSION:

THE KITCHEN -

is small with a window.

Cathy begins to boil water in the kettle. She then walks to the window and opens it.

CATHY'S P.O.V. - LOOKING OUT THE WINDOW

There is a car passing by and children are waiting for the school bus.

RETURN TO SCENE

Use Only Courier Typeface

This example is typed in 12-point Times, the common default font in many word-processing programs. This proportional typeface takes considerably less space on the page than the non-proportional Courier.

- In this brief excerpt, the two additional lines (see below) that are gained by using Courier might seem insignificant. However, spread over the course of a 110-page, feature-length screenplay, the page count would be severely affected.

- If the entire screenplay were written in 12-point Times, it would run about 20 pages less than with 12-point Courier. The consequence would be to throw off the "one page of script equals one minute of screen time" guide, which is still the current standard.

The only appropriate typeface for a screenplay is 12-point Courier.

A CORRECTED VERSION:

```
THE KITCHEN -

is small with a window.

Cathy begins to boil water in the kettle.  She then walks to
the window and opens it.

CATHY'S P.O.V. - LOOKING OUT THE WINDOW

There is a car passing by and children are waiting for the
school bus.

RETURN TO SCENE
```

CONFUSING REAL TIME AND SCREEN TIME

Real time refers to the actual time that an event would take when witnessed in the physical world. *Screen time* is used to designate the time that the event takes when viewed in the movie.

- Because time in the physical world is constant, it must include all those time-consuming elements that have no bearing on the story being told.

- In a movie, the goal is to eliminate those patches of real time that have no narrative value and do not affect either the plot or the characters. Thus, most screen time compresses real time into dramatic units.

THE ORIGINAL VERSION:

```
INT.  REBECCA'S KITCHEN - MORNING

The kitchen is small and run down.  There is a window above
the sink.
```

```
Rebecca enters and runs water into a kettle.  She places the
kettle on the stove top and turns on the heat.

Rebecca goes to the refrigerator and takes out an English
muffin.  She places it in the toaster oven.  From the cabinet,
she takes out a tea bag and places it in an empty mug.

After a few minutes, the kettle begins to WHISTLE and she
quickly removes it from the stove.  She then pours the boiling
water into the mug.  After she has filled the mug, she puts
the kettle back down and goes over to the toaster oven where
she removes the muffin and places it on a plate.  She reaches
over to where the mug is and grabs it.  She takes a spoon and
lifts the tea bag from the boiling water, then winds the
string from the bag to get the last drops.  Satisfied, she
throws out the used tea bag in the waste basket beneath the
sink.  She takes the tea cup and muffin plate to the table.

Looking out the window, she sips her tea.
```

Be Aware of Screen Time

Aside from all the unnecessary detail, the writer specifically informs us "After a few minutes, the kettle begins to whistle . . ." Are we really going to wait the *few minutes* it takes for the water to boil? In real time, this would certainly be accurate; in screen time, however, these few minutes would be deadly.

You need to find a way of compressing time. Fortunately, several conventions can be used to do this.

A CORRECTED VERSION:

```
INT. REBECCA'S KITCHEN - MORNING

The kitchen is small and run down.  There is a window above
the sink.  Rebecca enters.

She runs water into a kettle, places it on the stove and turns
on the heat.  She next takes out an English muffin from the
refrigerator and puts it in the toaster oven.  Moving to the
window, she looks outside.

REBECCA'S P.O.V. - THE NEIGHBORHOOD

It's a lovely summer day.  Children are playing.  Neighbors
are working on their lawns.

The kettle WHISTLES as -

RETURN TO SCENE -

following Rebecca as she makes tea.
```

Explanation and Notes

By cinematic convention, if we leave a basic but lengthy activity (such as waiting for the kettle to boil or the muffin to heat) and then return to that activity, the real time it would take is compressed into a briefer amount of screen time.

Within a scene, there are several ways to compress real time into screen time.

- In the corrected version, the use of REBECCA'S P.O.V. allows us to slip away from the activity in the kitchen. Although the P.O.V. only takes a few seconds, when we return to the kitchen, the water is boiling.

  The P.O.V. allows real time to be compressed into screen time.

- This could also be accomplished by a CUTAWAY or an INTERCUT.

  Another way you could compress the time is to have Rebecca start the kettle and muffin and then walk into another room to do something. When she returns, the water is boiling and the muffin is toasted.

  Or you could organize the breakfast into a SERIES OF SHOTS and let the director manage the screen time.

Unless you have a particular reason for doing so, it is best to be vague about any length of real time in a screenplay. For example, "After a few minutes" might have been written as "Moments later".

Scene Line/Slug Line Mistakes

WRITING INACCURATE SCENE LINES

Because each scene begins with a scene line, it is critical to state the elements—setting, location, and time—clearly and accurately.

THE ORIGINAL VERSION:

```
EXT.  SALLY'S CAR - NIGHT (MOVING)

Sally is driving along in her brand new Honda Civic.  She sees
that the gas gauge is low.  She pulls into a service station.
She parks the car near a gas pump and gets out.  She notices a
sign that reads "Mechanic on Duty".
```

The Scene Line Must Accurately Define the Content of the Scene

The scene line defines the location as EXT. SALLY'S CAR, so that we are viewing her Honda Civic from the *outside* as she drives. But if we are outside the car, how can we know that Sally looks at the gas gauge and that the fuel is low?

If it is important to know that the reason Sally pulls into the gas station is that her gas is low, then we would need a view *inside* the car to be able to see the gas gauge.

This could be accomplished in one of several ways:

- One way to solve the scene line problem would be to change the scene line setting from EXT. to INT. You could then simply write what Sally sees into the instructions and let the director decide how to set the shot. You could use the EXT. when she pulls into the gas station.

A CORRECTED VERSION 1:

```
INT.   SALLY'S CAR - NIGHT (MOVING)

Sally is driving along in her brand new Honda Civic.  She sees
that the gas gauge is low.  She pulls into a service station.


EXT.   SERVICE STATION - CONTINUOUS

She parks the car near a gas pump and gets out.  She notices a
sign that reads "Mechanic on Duty".
```

- If it is critical to your narrative to have Sally looking at the gauge, you could use a slug line specifying SALLY'S P.O.V. Using the slug line would indicate to the reader that it is *very* important to know that she looks at the gas gauge.

A CORRECTED VERSION 2:

```
INT.   SALLY'S CAR - NIGHT (MOVING)

Sally is driving along in her brand new Honda Civic.  She
looks at the dashboard.

SALLY'S P.O.V. - THE GAS GAUGE

which is nearly empty.


EXT.   SERVICE STATION - CONTINUOUS

Sally pulls into a service station and parks the car near a
gas pump.  She gets out and notices a sign that reads
"Mechanic on Duty".
```

- Or it may be that we don't need to know that the gas tank is low. The fact that Sally pulls into a service station and stops at a fuel pump implies that she needs gas.

A CORRECTED VERSION 3:

```
EXT.   CITY STREETS - NIGHT (MOVING)

Sally is driving along in her brand new Honda Civic.  She
pulls into a service station.


EXT.   SERVICE STATION - CONTINUOUS

Parking her car near a gas pump, Sally gets out.  A sign reads
"Mechanic on Duty".
```

- Yet another solution could be to use an expanded scene line that would include both the interior of Sally's car and the exterior of the service station.

A CORRECTED VERSION 4:

```
INT./EXT.  SALLY'S CAR/SERVICE STATION - NIGHT

Sally is driving along in her brand new Honda Civic.  She sees
that the gas gauge is low.

She pulls into a service station.

Parking her car near a gas pump, Sally gets out.  A sign reads
"Mechanic on Duty".
```

CONFUSING SCENE LINES WITH SLUG LINES

Confusing scene lines with slug lines is a common problem because the two look very similar and even share similar duties.

THE ORIGINAL VERSION:

```
FADE IN:

INT.  MARIA'S APARTMENT - MORNING

MASTER BEDROOM

MARIA, in her mid to late twenties with black hair, is
sleeping under the covers in her bed.  A loud KNOCK on the
door.

Maria continues to sleep.  As the KNOCKING gets louder, she
slowly wakes from her sleep.

Finally she gets out of bed, adjusts her tee-shirt and boxers,
and quickly walks out of the room.


INT.  MARIA'S LIVING ROOM - CONTINUOUS

As she walks to the front door, the phone RINGS.
```

Use Scene Lines and Slug Lines with Consistency and Efficiency

All scene lines and many slug lines are used to define spatial locations. Beyond this similarity, their applications are quite different. You can't mix-and-match scene lines and slug lines to define locations as if they were interchangeable.

A *scene line* defines the location of the master shot; among other functions, a *slug line* can specify a particular area within the master shot.

- In the previous example, the scene line INT. MARIA'S APARTMENT informs us that Maria's apartment, which includes several rooms, will serve as the location for the scene. Slug lines are required to subdivide the apartment into the various rooms— MASTER BEDROOM, LIVING ROOM, KITCHEN.

  Further, it is inconsistent to use INT. MARIA'S APARTMENT for one scene (with a slug line specifying the MASTER BEDROOM) and then to use INT. MARIA'S LIVING ROOM for the next scene.

- One solution would be to treat each room as a separate scene.

A CORRECTED VERSION 1:

```
FADE IN:

INT. MARIA'S BEDROOM - MORNING

MARIA, in her mid to late twenties with black hair, is
sleeping under the covers in her bed.  A loud KNOCK on the
door.

Maria continues to sleep.  As the KNOCKING gets louder, she
slowly wakes from her sleep.

Finally she gets out of bed, adjusts her tee-shirt and boxers,
and quickly walks out of the room.


INT. MARIA'S LIVING ROOM - CONTINUOUS

She walks to the front door, the phone RINGS.
```

- Although making each room into its own scene fixes the initial problem, it splits the apartment into fragments.

  A cleaner solution would be to consider MARIA'S APARTMENT as the scene line and to use slug lines to indicate the individual rooms. This is more like the way viewers would follow it in the film, seeing the apartment as unified.

A CORRECTED VERSION 2:

```
FADE IN:

INT. MARIA'S APARTMENT - MORNING

MASTER BEDROOM

MARIA, in her mid to late twenties with black hair, is
sleeping under the covers in her bed.  A loud KNOCK on the
door.

Maria continues to sleep.  As the KNOCKING gets louder, she
slowly wakes from her sleep.
```

```
Finally she gets out of bed, adjusts her tee-shirt and boxers,
and quickly walks out of the room into the -

LIVING ROOM

She walks to the front door.  The phone RINGS.
```

CONFUSING LOCATIONS

A scene line that defines a structure (an apartment, a school, an office, etc.) that is subdivided into various rooms must be carefully segmented by slug lines to allow the reader to visualize what is happening. It is easy to get sloppy when moving from room to room.

THE ORIGINAL VERSION:

```
INT.   CAROLINE'S APARTMENT - DAY

Caroline, wearing a bathrobe, is carefully applying make-up.
She is nervous and moody.  Jonathan is casually lounging on
the bed.

                    CAROLINE
          What should I wear?  What kind of look
          are they after?

Caroline continues with her make-up.

                    CAROLINE (cont'd)
          I think I'm nervous.

                    JONATHAN
          Don't worry.  You'll be fine.

                    CAROLINE
               (moving into view)
          Well, how do I look?

Caroline comes out wearing a black jumpsuit.

                    JONATHAN
               (impressed)
          You look great!
```

Use Slug Lines to Partition a Structure into Its Component Rooms

In this example, because there are no slug lines subdividing the apartment, we are never clear where Caroline is when applying her make-up and where Jonathan is waiting for her.

- According to the way in which the scene opens, Caroline is in view as she is applying her make-up.

  However, the parenthetical (moving into view) contradicts that, informing us that she was previously out of view. Caroline's dialogue to John—"Well, how do I look?"—followed by the description of her clothing would certainly indicate that this is the first time we see her. (Was she behind a screen or in an adjacent bathroom?)

- If this is indeed the first time Caroline appears in the scene, then her previous dialogue would have to be (O.S.).

A CORRECTED VERSION:

```
INT.  CAROLINE'S APARTMENT - DAY

BATHROOM

Caroline, wearing a bathrobe, is carefully applying make-up.
She is nervous and moody.

                    CAROLINE
          What should I wear?  What kind of look
          are they after?

Caroline continues with her make-up.

BEDROOM

Jonathan is casually lounging on the bed.

                    CAROLINE (O.S.)(cont'd)
          I think I'm nervous.

                    JONATHAN
          Don't worry.  You'll be fine.

                    CAROLINE (O.S.)
          Well, how do I look?

Caroline enters the bedroom, now wearing a black jumpsuit.

                    JONATHAN
          You look great!
```

IMPROPER INTERCUTTING OF VISUALS

The INTERCUT AS NEEDED device can be very useful in a screenplay. However, it can also cause problems when it is not carefully applied.

THE ORIGINAL VERSION:

```
INT.  JENNA'S HOUSE - DAY

Jenna races to the phone and dials.


INT.  POLICE PRECINCT STATION - CONTINUOUS

Amid the flurry of activity, the Desk Sergeant answers the
phone.

INTERCUT AS NEEDED

                    DESK SERGEANT
          Forty-first precinct.  Officer Mullin.

Jenna paces back and forth.

                    JENNA
               (into phone; frantic)
          I was watching TV, and I suddenly
          heard a woman scream.  Then I heard
          a thud.  Like something really heavy
          hit the ground.

The Desk Sergeant is writing the information on pad.

                    DESK SERGEANT
          Okay, I'm going to send someone over
          to look into it.  What's the address?
               (pause; writing)
          Can you give me a description of your
          neighbor?
               (pause; writing)
          Okay, I'll try to get someone there as
          soon as possible.

RETURN TO SCENE

Jenna hangs up the phone and lights a cigarette, taking
frantic and deep puffs.
```

Use Intercutting Only When Controlling the Visuals Is Not Necessary

It is a common practice to intercut between the parties during a phone conversation.

- The INTERCUT AS NEEDED assumes that it is not essential to the narrative which visual is on screen at any given moment.

- The main advantage of using INTERCUT is to eliminate moving back-and-forth using slug lines. Preserving the phone conversation keeps the attention on the dialogue.

There are three basic considerations in using the INTERCUT convention:

- First, both locations need to be clearly identified. In the preceding example, both Jenna's house and the police precinct have been described.

  If these locations have not been previously described, you will need to do that before the INTERCUT can be used.

- Second, when the Desk Sergeant asks Jenna for a description, the parenthetical (pause) indicates that we do not hear Jenna's response. This violates the intention of the intercut convention, which allows us to hear both sides of the conversation without regard to the visuals.

  If the writer needs to have the visuals stay on the Desk Sergeant, then a slug line such as POLICE PRECINCT or DESK SERGEANT would be required.

- Third, when the intercut is finished, you need to terminate it with either a slug line or a transition.

A CORRECTED VERSION:

```
INT.  JENNA'S HOUSE - DAY

Jenna races to the phone and dials.


INT.  POLICE PRECINCT STATION - CONTINUOUS

Amid the flurry of activity, the DESK SERGEANT answers the
phone.

                    DESK SERGEANT
          Forty-first precinct.  Officer Mullin.

INTERCUT AS NEEDED - JENNA AND SERGEANT ON PHONE

                    JENNA
               (frantic)
          I was watching TV, and I suddenly
          heard a woman scream.  Then I heard
          a thud.  Like something really heavy
          hit the ground.

                    DESK SERGEANT
          Okay, I'm going to send someone over
          to look into it.  What's the address?

                    JENNA
          6810 Maynada.  Please hurry.

                    DESK SERGEANT
          Can you give me a description of your
          neighbor?

                    JENNA
          She's an older woman, maybe sixty or
          so, overweight.  Usually wears a kind of
          muu-muu.
```

```
                      DESK SERGEANT
                     (still writing)
          Okay, I'll try to get someone there as
          soon as possible.

JENNA'S LIVING ROOM

Jenna hangs up the phone and lights a cigarette, taking
frantic and deep puffs.
```

Explanation and Notes

The principal advantage to the INTERCUT AS NEEDED slug line is to keep the phone conversation intact—uninterrupted with either scene lines or slug lines that would otherwise separate the locations and participants.

In this example, the usual parenthetical (into phone) is omitted because the slug line specifies that it is all a phone conversation and neither Jenna nor the Sergeant speak to anyone else.

CONFUSING SLUG LINES

As a descriptive tool, slug lines can be an invaluable asset for the screenwriter. But when slug lines are inappropriately or carelessly applied, they can cause confusion and frustration for the reader.

THE ORIGINAL VERSION:

```
INT.  GEORGE'S LIVING ROOM - DAY

George's face looks shocked and disheartened as he scans the
ransacked room.  Books are on the floor, the sofa has been
taken apart.  The room is a mess.

Every plant has been removed from its pot, the soil carelessly
dumped in little piles on his white carpet.

George wanders around and inspects the damage.  He stops at
the window to re-pot a vine-like hanging plant.  While in the
process of hanging the pot from a ceiling hook, he looks out
the window.

MARY JANE

George sees MARY JANE, a drop-dead gorgeous woman in her early
twenties.  She is moving in next door.

She is carrying several potted plants.

RETURN TO SCENE
```

Use the Correct Slug Line

The intent of the slug line MARY JANE is to inform us that George watches Mary Jane from his window as she moves her potted plants. But there are two basic problems with the slug line MARY JANE:

- Even though Mary Jane is the object of our vision, the line of sight belongs to George. Therefore, the slug line MARY JANE needs to be changed to indicate that it is George who is looking at Mary Jane.

- Further, leaving the slug line as MARY JANE erroneously informs the reader that the scene shifts from inside George's living room to outside, where Mary Jane is carrying the plants. This would require a new scene.

However, using the correct slug line would resolve the confusion:

GEORGE'S P.O.V. - OUT THE WINDOW

A CORRECTED VERSION:

```
INT.  GEORGE'S LIVING ROOM - DAY

George's face looks shocked and disheartened as he scans the
ransacked room.  Books are on the floor, the sofa has been
taken apart.  The room is a mess.

Every plant has been removed from its pot, the soil carelessly
dumped in little piles on his white carpet.

George wanders around and inspects the damage.  He stops at
the window to re-pot a vine-like hanging plant.  While in the
process of hanging the pot from a ceiling hook, he looks out
the window.

GEORGE'S P.O.V. - OUT THE WINDOW

MARY JANE, a drop-dead gorgeous woman in her twenties, is
moving in next door.

She is carrying several potted plants.

RETURN TO SCENE
```

CREATING UNCLEAR CUTAWAYS

Cutaways can be a very useful tool for the screenwriter. But when misused, they can create problems for the reader.

THE ORIGINAL VERSION:

```
INT.  JAMIE'S BEDROOM - EVENING

The phone RINGS.  Jamie picks it up.
```

```
                    JAMIE
               (into phone)
          Hello.

CUTAWAY - KAREN

                    KAREN
               (into phone; nervously)
          Jamie, is that you?

INTERCUT AS NEEDED - JAMIE AND KAREN ON PHONE

                    JAMIE
               (into phone)
          Yeah.  Who is this?  Marie?

                    KAREN
               (into phone)
          No, honey.  It's Karen.  I'm in
          the city.  I need a favor.
```

Note: This phone conversation between Jamie and Karen continues beyond what is included in this box. The example is for the CUTAWAY, not the intercutting.

Specify the Environment for the Cutaway

- The CUTAWAY is a visual slug line. Unless it is obvious from the context (a previous scene or situation) where Karen is when she makes the phone call, the cutaway needs a brief statement identifying that location. This could be as brief as, for example, a phone booth or her car.

  If, in a previous scene, it has already been made clear where Karen is, then KAREN ON PHONE would be appropriate.

- Further, the scene line informs us that the primary scene is JAMIE'S BEDROOM and the secondary scene is KAREN ON PHONE. We would expect that after the phone conversation concludes, the scene would return to Jamie in her bedroom.

A CORRECTED VERSION:

```
INT.  JAMIE'S BEDROOM - EVENING

The phone RINGS.  Jamie picks it up.

                    JAMIE
               (into phone)
          Hello?

CUTAWAY - KAREN ON PHONE

She is in a phone booth in a CROWDED bar.
```

> KAREN
> (nervously)
> Jamie, is that you?
>
> INTERCUT AS NEEDED - JAMIE AND KAREN ON PHONE
>
> JAMIE
> Yeah. Who is this? Marie?
>
> KAREN
> No, honey. It's Karen. I'm in
> the city. I need a favor.

Explanation and Notes

In this corrected version, once the slug lines include the instruction ON PHONE, it is not necessary to have the parenthetical (into phone). Therefore, all dialogue is assumed to be spoken over the phone.

USING THE INCORRECT FORMAT FOR A SERIES OF SHOTS

A SERIES OF SHOTS has a designated format that must be followed.

THE ORIGINAL VERSION:

> EXT.   AFFLUENT SUBURBAN NEIGHBORHOOD - DAY
>
> The sun is shining brightly on the rows of pretty houses.
>
> SERIES OF SHOTS - Neighbors are outside. Some are sitting on porches. Others are washing cars and tending to lawns. A couple of joggers pass by. And children are playing badminton.
>
> The POSTAL TRUCK appears, slows and stops at one of the houses.

Fix the Series of Shots

You must use the standard A. B. C. itemization for a series. Remember that a series must be:

- Introduced by a slug line (which includes a brief explanation of their unity).

- Presented as a list (A., B., C., etc.).

- Written in regular mixed case. (If it is presented in all caps, it looks too much like a slug line, which it is not.)

A CORRECTED VERSION:

```
EXT.  AFFLUENT SUBURBAN NEIGHBORHOOD - DAY

The sun is shining brightly on the rows of pretty houses.

SERIES OF SHOTS - THE NEIGHBORHOOD

A.  NEIGHBORS are outside.  Some are sitting on porches while
others are washing cars and tending to lawns.

B.  A couple of JOGGERS pass by.

C.  CHILDREN are playing badminton.

RETURN TO SCENE

The POSTAL TRUCK appears, slows and stops at one of the
houses.
```

AN ALTERNATIVE

The above SERIES OF SHOTS could also be written as simple instructions. For example:

```
EXT.  AFFLUENT SUBURBAN NEIGHBORHOOD - DAY

The sun is shining brightly on the rows of pretty houses.
NEIGHBORS are outside in front of their homes.  Some are
sitting on their porches, some are tending to their lawns,
and some are washing cars.  A couple of JOGGERS.  CHILDREN
are playing badminton.

The POSTAL TRUCK appears, slows and stops at one of the
houses.
```

The decision to present the description about the neighborhood as a series of shots or as instructions will be determined by the importance of the information.

- If, for example, the neighbors, children, and joggers turn out to be major elements in the story, then you might want to bring attention to them in a series of shots.

- But if this is simply introductory background, then a series of shots may draw too much attention to the individual items.

Instruction Mistakes

WRITING INSTRUCTIONS IN THE PAST TENSE

It is common in literary writing to use the past tense for descriptions. Screenwriting, however, follows a strict convention for describing the events of a scene as they occur.

THE ORIGINAL VERSION:

```
EXT.  GAS STATION - DAY

Rebecca pulled into the gas station, next to a pump.  She shut
off her car engine, got out of the car, removed the nozzle
from the pump, swiped the credit card and inserted the nozzle
into the tank.  She then started the pump.

REBECCA'S P.O.V. - SIGN ON GAS PUMPS

She noticed a sign reading "Mechanic on Duty".

RETURN TO SCENE

The gas pump clicked off, Rebecca removed the nozzle and
returned it to the slot in the pump.
```

Adjust the Verb Tense

Because a movie is always occurring as we experience it, the *instructions* in a screenplay are ALWAYS written in the *present tense.*

- Regardless of whether the narrative takes place in the past, present, or future, be careful to keep all instructions in the present tense.

- In *dialogue*, characters may use the past or future tense.

A CORRECTED VERSION:

```
EXT.  GAS STATION - DAY

Rebecca pulls into the gas station, next to a pump.  She shuts
off her car engine, gets out of the car, removes the nozzle
from the pump, swipes the credit card and inserts the nozzle
into the tank.  She then starts the pump.

REBECCA'S P.O.V. - SIGN ON GAS PUMPS

She notices a sign reading "Mechanic on Duty".

RETURN TO SCENE

The gas pump clicks off, Rebecca removes the nozzle and
returns it to the slot in the pump.
```

USING ILLOGICAL WORDING

Bad wording can be a problem in any mode of writing.

THE ORIGINAL VERSION:

> Several people stand in front of the small hut holding strange
> looking spears dressed in loin cloths.

Adjust the Sentence Structure

As written, the sentence in this example informs us that the *spears* are dressed in loin cloths, not the people. A simple re-wording will eliminate the unintentional humor.

A CORRECTED VERSION:

> Several people dressed in loin cloths and holding strange
> looking spears stand in front of the small hut.

USING ILLOGICAL ACTIONS

Characters in screenplays can only do what you instruct them to do. You can't assume that they will act without your guidance.

THE ORIGINAL VERSION:

> INT. STEFAN'S OFFICE - CONTINUOUS
>
> Angela enters the office.
>
> The office is neat and clean. STEFAN is a handsome man in
> his early forties. He is sitting at his desk. It is very
> orderly. He barely looks up from his paperwork. He motions
> to her to take a seat opposite the desk.
>
>   STEFAN
>   Can I get you a drink?
>
>   ANGELA
>   Yes. Diet Coke, please.
>
>   STEFAN
>   (opening a can)
>   Tell me what you know about the part.
>
>   ANGELA
>   (sipping the Coke)
>   Well, it's a small . . .

> STEFAN
> (interrupting; annoyed)
> There are no small parts in my movies.

Clearly Describe the Actions of the Characters

The actions described in this scene were very carelessly written.

- Although Stefan motions for Angela to take a seat, the writer has neglected to have her sit.

  As written, it is unclear whether Angela sits or remains standing.

- Unless the desk has a concealed mini-fridge, Stefan needs to get up and walk to a fridge before he can get the Diet Coke.

  Assuming that there is a fridge in the office, it needs to be mentioned when describing the office.

- The parentheticals add to the confusion.

  How did Angela get the drink? Did Stefan hand it to her? And has Stefan returned to his seat?

A CORRECTED VERSION:

INT.   STEFAN'S OFFICE - CONTINUOUS

Angela enters the office.

The office is neat and clean with several chairs and a
mini-fridge to one side.   Posters of B-level exploitation
movies adorn the walls.

STEFAN, a handsome man in his early forties, is sitting at his
very orderly desk.   He barely looks up from his paperwork as
he motions to her to take a seat opposite the desk.

> STEFAN
> (looking up)
> Can I get you a drink?

Angela sits.

> ANGELA
> Yes.   Diet Coke, please.

Stefan gets up and walks to the fridge.   As he retrieves a
Coke from the fridge -

> STEFAN
> Tell me what you know about the part.

Stefan walks over to Angela and hands her the Coke.   Angela's
eyes follow him as he resumes his seat.

```
                            ANGELA
                      (sipping the Coke)
                  Well, it's a small . . .

                            STEFAN
                    (interrupting; annoyed)
                  There are no small parts in my movies.
```

A Note about Writing Style

In the original version, the short sentences describing Stefan and his activities are a series of simple, repetitious sentences.

- Such blandness in writing risks becoming dull and tedious to the reader.

- By varying the sentence structure, you can make the piece more interesting.

CAPPING WORDS EXCESSIVELY

The use of words and phrases that are written with each letter capitalized (called CAPS or CAPPING) has a specific function in screenwriting. CAPPING is used to announce scene lines, slug lines, and transitions.

In the instructions, words and phrases are CAPPED because they have a particular significance and the reader's eye is drawn to them. When capping is abused, however, the significance becomes lost or confused.

THE ORIGINAL VERSION:

```
It's RAINING.  Elliott is soaking WET, wearing a TEE-SHIRT and
JEANS.  He finds some shelter at the CORNER of a building.  He
comes out from behind the BUILDING and walks by people wearing
TRENCH COATS and carrying UMBRELLAS.  The people give Elliott
weird looks as he passes them.  He continues on to a BUS
STOP.  A BUS pulls up and Elliott gets on.
```

Cap Only Words and Phrases That Have Narrative Significance

It is evident from scanning the above paragraph that capping too many words defeats the entire purpose of capping, which is to inform the reader that something is ESSENTIAL to the narrative or the character.

- Because RAINING, WET, TEE-SHIRT, JEANS, CORNER, BUILDING, TRENCH COATS, UMBRELLAS, BUS STOP, and BUS have no effect on the story, none of these should be capped.

- Ironically, the only word in the entire paragraph that *must* be capped is not. The word PEOPLE must be capped because it identifies a group that is being introduced.

If the inclement weather is important to the narrative, then RAINING also should be capped. The production team would outfit the characters appropriately.

A CORRECTED VERSION:

> It's RAINING. Elliott is soaking wet, wearing a tee-shirt and jeans. He finds some shelter at the corner of a building.
>
> He comes out from behind the building and walks by PEOPLE wearing trench coats and carrying umbrellas. The people give Elliott weird looks as he passes them.
>
> Elliott continues on to a bus stop.

PROVIDING UNKNOWABLE INFORMATION

A novel or short story can freely provide the reader with expository and editorial information whenever it is convenient, A screenplay, however, is severely restricted in what can be revealed.

To go beyond what can be seen and heard on the screen violates what the medium can do.

THE ORIGINAL VERSION:

> INT.   SAM'S TAXI - DAWN (MOVING)
>
> Sam looks at his watch and sees that it's getting late.
>
>   SAM
>   Time to call it a night.
>
> He's thinking of his kids. His wife will be waiting for him with the usual coffee and toast.

Use Visual References to Suggest Information and Feelings

In this scene, the writer tells us two things about Sam that we cannot possibly know:

- Sam looks at his watch, but then the writer *tells* us what looking at the watch means to Sam. We can see Sam look at his watch, but we have no way of knowing "that it's getting late." Therefore, that information cannot be stated in the instructions.

  This problem is easily solved. After Sam looks at his watch, a visual reaction—a yawn or stretch—would suggest that it's late. Adding a parenthetical (yawning) or (stretching) to the dialogue would make Sam's condition even clearer.

- Similarly, in the paragraph following Sam's dialogue, we are informed that he is thinking of what awaits him at home.

For this problem, there are several possible solutions: One would be to have Sam look at a photograph of his family and suggest by his reaction how he is longing to get home.

Another possibility would be to inject a brief visual of what Sam is anticipating at home. This option would require providing a slug line and description of what he expects.

Because movies are visual rather than literary, a screenwriter can use looks, mannerisms, gestures, and reactions to imply what a novelist might simply state in words.

A CORRECTED VERSION 1:

```
INT.   SAM'S TAXI - DAWN (MOVING)

Sam looks at his watch.  He yawns and stretches out one arm
while keeping the other on the steering wheel.

                    SAM
          Time to call it a night.

Sam looks up at the PHOTOGRAPH attached to his visor.  It's a
nice domestic portrait of his Wife and Children.
```

A CORRECTED VERSION 2:

```
INT.   SAM'S TAXI - DAWN (MOVING)

Sam looks at his watch.  He yawns and stretches out one arm
while keeping the other on the steering wheel.

                    SAM
                 (fatigued)
          Time to call it a night.

SAM'S DAYDREAM - HOME

The Children are just waking.  His Wife is waiting for him
with coffee and toast.

RETURN TO SCENE
```

PROVIDING A PREMATURE DESCRIPTION

It is inappropriate to provide a description of a character before he or she is visually present.

THE ORIGINAL VERSION:

```
INT.  MIKE'S APARTMENT - MORNING

THE BEDROOM

A loud DOORBELL.  Again, a DOORBELL.

Waking up, Mike gets out of bed and staggers into -

THE LIVING ROOM

KEVIN, twenty, is dressed in baggy jeans, tee-shirt and a
baseball cap worn backward.

Mike unlocks and opens the door, and Kevin enters.
```

Describe Characters at the Appropriate Times

Because the scene line informs us that we are *inside* Mike's apartment, we would not be able to see Kevin, who is *outside* the apartment. Therefore, Kevin cannot be described until Mike opens the door.

There are several possible solutions to this problem:

- One easy fix would be to simply switch the last two paragraphs. We would then see Kevin when the door has been opened.

A CORRECTED VERSION 1:

```
INT.  MIKE'S APARTMENT - MORNING

THE BEDROOM

A loud DOORBELL.  Again, a DOORBELL.

Waking up, Mike gets out of bed and staggers into -

THE LIVING ROOM -

and approaches the front door.  Mike unlocks and opens the
door.

KEVIN, twenty, enters.  He is dressed in baggy jeans,
tee-shirt and a baseball cap worn backward.
```

- One alternate would be to insert a scene in the hallway, in which Kevin is introduced as he rings the doorbell, and then to cut back to Mike's apartment as Mike answers the door.

A CORRECTED VERSION 2:

```
INT.  MIKE'S APARTMENT - MORNING

THE BEDROOM

A loud DOORBELL.  Again, a DOORBELL.

Waking up, Mike gets out of bed and staggers out the bedroom
into -

THE LIVING ROOM -

and approaches the front door.


INT.  HALLWAY, OUTSIDE MIKE'S APARTMENT - CONTINUOUS

KEVIN, twenty, is dressed in baggy jeans, tee-shirt and a
baseball cap worn backward.


INT.  MIKE'S APARTMENT - CONTINUOUS

THE LIVING ROOM

Mike unlocks and opens the door.  Kevin enters.
```

- Another solution would be to use an expanded scene line to include both the inside and outside of Mike's apartment and slug lines to move between the two locations.

A CORRECTED VERSION 3:

```
INT.  MIKE'S APARTMENT/OUTSIDE HALLWAY - MORNING

THE BEDROOM

A loud DOORBELL.  Again, a DOORBELL.

Waking up, Mike gets out of bed and staggers out the bedroom
into -

THE LIVING ROOM -

and approaches the front door.

OUTSIDE HALLWAY

KEVIN, twenty, is dressed in baggy jeans, tee-shirt and a
baseball cap worn backward.  He rings the doorbell again.
```

```
THE LIVING ROOM

Mike unlocks and opens the door.  Kevin enters.
```

OVER-DESCRIBING A BASIC ACTIVITY

Providing excessively detailed descriptions for familiar activities can devour pages and subvert, rather than enhance, the narrative.

THE ORIGINAL VERSION:

```
INT.  REBECCA'S KITCHEN - MORNING

The kitchen is small and run down.  There is a window above
the sink.

Rebecca enters and runs water into a kettle.  She places the
kettle on the stove top and turns on the heat.

Rebecca goes to the refrigerator and takes out an English
muffin.  She places it in the toaster oven.  From the cabinet,
she takes out a tea bag and places it in an empty mug.

The kettle begins to WHISTLE and she quickly removes it from
the stove.  She then pours the boiling water into the mug.
After she has filled the mug, she puts the kettle back down
and makes her way over to the toaster oven where she removes
the muffin and places it on a plate.  She reaches over to
where the mug is and grabs it.  She takes a spoon and lifts
the tea bag from the boiling water, then winds the string from
the bag to get the last drops.  Satisfied, she throws out the
used tea bag in the waste basket beneath the sink.  She takes
the tea cup and muffin plate to the table.

Looking out the window, she sips her tea.
```

Describe a Basic Activity in Limited Detail

This is a frequent mistake by beginning screenwriters. How much detail is enough? Providing too much information about an activity eats up a lot of lines on the page and risks losing the reader's attention.

- Unless there is some specific reason for describing every tiny action, the level of detail shown in the previous example is far too much for a simple act such as making breakfast.

  You might ask yourself, What is important in this activity?

- Assuming that the details of Rebecca's breakfast are not critical to the narrative, a cleaner version might reduce the description to its simplest form. This would allow the director to decide on the details.

The point here is to avoid description and detail that is inconsequential to the narrative. Lengthy passages like the one about Rebecca's breakfast will either mislead the reader (who will assume that something pertinent to the narrative is happening) or bore the reader (by bogging down the reading with superfluous material).

A CORRECTED VERSION:

```
INT. REBECCA'S KITCHEN - MORNING

The kitchen is small and run down with a window above the
sink.

Rebecca enters.  She routinely makes a modest breakfast of
tea and a muffin.
```

NEGLECTING AN IMPORTANT DESCRIPTION

We infer a great deal from what we see. So, when a character appears in a space that is personal, we consider how he or she furnishes and decorates that environment as a reflection of the character's personality.

THE ORIGINAL VERSION:

```
INT.  ANGELA'S APARTMENT - DAY

In the living room, Angela is at the CD rack searching through
the albums.

When she finds a particular title, she takes the disc out and
puts it into the player.  She uses the remote control to
listen to the first moments of THREE SONGS.

On the next try, she leaves the FOURTH SONG playing while she
rushes into -

THE BEDROOM -

where she stops in front of the mirror and begins to improvise
a sensual dance to the music.
```

Use Description to Establish Character

Because this is the first time we see Angela, the main character, in her residence, it is very important to describe her environment more completely. In part, Angela's personality will be revealed by how she decorates and arranges her most private and personal space.

- The paragraph describing her living room tells us only that Angela has a CD collection and player. Is there anything distinctive about the room? Are there decorations on the walls? If so, are they posters of rock concerts or prints of classic paintings? Are there personal effects, such as photographs and trinkets, that reflect her life?

  Further, the paragraph tells us nothing about the condition of the room. For example, is it clean or messy? Is it maintained or dilapidated? Are the purchased items cheap, basic, or extravagant? Describing the living room, even with a few details, can help us determine Angela's interests, tastes, habits, and economic level.

  The point is, you never want to miss an opportunity to use décor and props to help define character.

- This does not mean that each and every item in the room must be inventoried.

  We can assume that a living room will have a sofa, a few chairs, a television, a telephone, a window, and floor or ceiling lamps.

  However, if there is anything distinctive about any of these (such as a huge, expensive television) that pertains to the narrative or the character, then it needs to be mentioned.

A CORRECTED VERSION:

```
INT.   ANGELA'S APARTMENT - DAY

In the living room, Angela is at the CD rack searching through
the albums.

Covering a large amount of the wall is a huge KISS poster.
Next to the poster is a large photograph of Tom Selleck and
Gene Simmons signed "To Angela with love, Gene."

Aside from an elaborate sound system for the stereo, the rest
of the room is ordinary.

When she finds a particular title, she takes the disc out and
puts it into the player.  She uses the remote control to
listen to the first moments of THREE SONGS.

On the next try, she leaves the FOURTH SONG playing while she
rushes into -

THE BEDROOM -

where she stops in front of a full-length wall mirror and
begins to improvise a sensual dance to the music.

This room has no furniture at all, except for a large mattress
on the floor.  It is as though she wants it to be a dance
studio, white on white with mirrors.
```

INTRODUCING TOO MANY CHARACTERS TOO QUICKLY

How and when to introduce the characters who will populate your screenplay is critical. If the reader is barraged with a rapid series of introductions, it will be difficult to remember the names and descriptions.

THE ORIGINAL VERSION:

```
In the center of the room, sitting in a circle of folding
chairs, are thirteen women, ranging in age, appearance, and
color.  There is ANDIE, thirty-five, frumpy and intellectual.
To her right is SAM who looks to be around the same age and is
tall, thin, prissy with long red hair and nerdy glasses.
JAMIE, a cheer-leader type in her late twenties, is seated
next to LINDSEY, a lanky model-type in her late twenties.
BRET, mid-thirties with long dark hair, who looks like a
female bodybuilder.  She sits with C.J., a feminine
professional woman in her mid-thirties.  TERRIE, a good-
looking African-American in her early thirties, and CHRIS,
mid-thirties and attractive stocky Latino woman who carries
herself like a cop.  PAT and LESLEY, both overweight women,
are in their late thirties, in leather biker outfits and
boots.  KYLE, a thin blonde librarian type and BLAIR, a
slightly butch-looking intellectual with short hair.  Sitting
alone is BOBBI, late thirties, broad and tall, who looks like
a man in drag.  There is one empty seat separating Bobbi from
the group.

Andie calls the meeting to order.
```

Introduce Characters as a Group

In this one paragraph, 13 women are introduced, each with a name and description. Cramming so many characters into such a compressed space renders each character equally important and difficult to recall.

Several options are available to resolve this problem:

- One solution would be to simply decide which characters need to be named and described. Perhaps only a few have any future importance to the screenplay. The rest could be collectively introduced as, for example, OTHER WOMEN or SIX OTHER WOMEN.

  By introducing (naming and describing) only those characters who will reappear and affect the story, you indicate to the reader which ones to remember.

- Another solution would be to reserve the introduction of each character until each speaks or acts. This would still be a large number of names and descriptions, but at least the introductions would be dispersed over the course of the scene.

- A third solution would be to introduce each woman by a distinctive characteristic, rather than a formal name. For example, Andie could be referred to as FRUMPY GIRL, Sam as PRISSY GIRL, Jamie as CHEERLEADER, and so forth. This has the advantage of fixing a certain look to each character, rather than just a name.

A CORRECTED VERSION:

> In the center of the room, sitting in a circle of folding chairs, are thirteen women, ranging in age, appearance, and color. They are randomly AD LIBBING about the weather, clothing, children and social duties.
>
> Clearly leading the group is ANDIE, thirty-five, frumpy and intellectual. She is dressed in a carefully matched spring blouse and skirt combination.
>
> Andie loudly clears her throat to get the ladies' attention. The cross-talk subsides as -
>
> ANDIE
> (politely)
> Thank you, thank you. I would like to introduce the group to Chris.
>
> Andie gestures to CHRIS, a mid-thirties and attractive stocky woman who carries herself like a cop.
>
> CHRIS
> (nervous)
> Thanks, Andie. I don't know why I feel nervous. Actually, I've had a chance to meet a lot of you already.

Explanation and Notes

In the corrected version, other women could be introduced as they speak or react. Presenting them this way will make it much easier for the reader to keep track of who's who.

INTRODUCING A CHARACTER INCORRECTLY

Every character in a screenplay, regardless of importance, needs to be properly introduced.

THE ORIGINAL VERSION:

> FADE IN:
>
> INT. TAXI CAB - NIGHT (MOVING)
>
> Frank, the driver, scratches his crippled leg while he searches for a fare. He's cruising the arrivals area of the airport.

Properly Introduce Characters

In this example, the name FRANK must be capped because it signals the first time that we see him. Also, Frank is the main character, but we have no description of his appearance.

- What is his approximate age? What is his general appearance? Is there anything distinctive about him? What is his attitude?

  Without some visual details, we cannot imagine Frank as anything more than a throwaway character, who needs no description.

- The writer tells us that Frank has a crippled leg, but how can we know that when we only see him seated in his cab? All we can know at this point is that he scratches his leg.

  This is an occasion where the writer *cannot* reveal certain information about Frank (that he has a bad leg) until it can be seen.

A CORRECTED VERSION 1:

```
FADE IN:

INT.  TAXI CAB - NIGHT (MOVING)

FRANK, the driver, scratches his leg while he searches for a
fare.  In his early thirties with several days of facial
growth to accompany his shoulder-length hair, Frank looks
like a hippie era burn-out.  He wears a rumpled Hawaiian
shirt.

He's cruising the arrivals area of the airport.
```

In this version, Frank is adequately described. And other than a description of him scratching his leg, nothing is made of his disability.

A CORRECTED VERSION 2:

```
FADE IN:

INT.  TAXI CAB - NIGHT (MOVING)

FRANK, the driver, scratches his leg while he searches for a
fare.  In his early thirties with several days of facial
growth to accompany his shoulder-length hair, Frank looks
like a hippie era burn-out.  He wears a rumpled Hawaiian
shirt.

He's cruising the arrivals area of the airport.
```

```
EXT.  AIRPORT, CURBSIDE - CONTINUOUS

An elderly LADY with several pieces of bulky luggage hails
the taxi.  Frank pulls to a stop and gets out to help his fare
with her baggage.  As he moves around the taxi, he walks with
a pronounced LIMP.
```

In this second version, not only is Frank described but the condition of his leg is withheld until he gets out of the car and we see him walk.

NOTE: CAPPING A PHYSICAL CHARACTERISTIC

What you cap provides critical information to the reader.

- In the version above, LIMP is capped, signifying that Frank *must* walk with a limp.

  Describing such a characteristic sends a powerful signal to the reader, who now expects that the limp will have some importance to the narrative. If the limp has no bearing on the script, then the reader has been misled.

- If the word *limp* is not capped, it would be interpreted as a physical characteristic that will have no particular importance to the narrative.

NOT CLARIFYING WHO IS IN A SCENE

As the screenwriter, you need to inform the reader who is in the scene when it opens. To neglect this requires the reader to backtrack and re-visualize the scene.

THE ORIGINAL VERSION:

```
INT.  GROCERY STORE - NIGHT

Eugene is looking for something on the floor.  He finally
spots some broken glass, kneels down and picks it up.

While he is kneeling, a PISTOL is firmly pressed against the
back of his neck.  Not knowing what it is, Eugene freezes.

                    ROBBER'S VOICE
          Don't move.

The man CLICKS the GUN that is on the back of Eugene's neck.

We now see the robber.

                    ROBBER (cont'd)
          Now, get the cash from the register.
```

Clearly Describe Who Is in the Scene

From the scene line, the master shot is the entire grocery store. Even though Eugene should not see the robber enter, *we* should.

A CORRECTED VERSION 1:

```
INT.  GROCERY STORE - NIGHT

Eugene is looking for something on the floor.

The ROBBER, a teen-aged boy dressed in grungy jeans and a
torn sweatshirt, enters.  He pulls a PISTOL that's tucked
into his jeans and quietly walks up behind Eugene who is
kneeling to pick up some broken glass.

The Robber firmly presses the barrel of the pistol against
the back of Eugene's neck.  Eugene freezes.

                         ROBBER
              Don't move.

The Robber CLICKS the hammer of the pistol.

                         ROBBER (cont'd)
              Now, get the cash from the register.
```

In this version, the scene is constructed as a master shot in which we see the robber but Eugene does not.

A CORRECTED VERSION 2:

```
INT.  GROCERY STORE - NIGHT

Eugene is looking for something on the floor.  He spots some
broken glass and kneels down to pick it up.

EUGENE

While kneeling, the BARREL of a pistol is firmly pressed
against the back of his neck.  Eugene freezes.

                         ROBBER'S VOICE (O.S.)
              Don't move.

The hammer of the pistol CLICKS, ready to fire.

RETURN TO SCENE

The ROBBER is a teen-aged boy dressed in grungy jeans and a
torn sweatshirt.

                         ROBBER (cont'd)
              Now, get the cash from the register.
```

Assuming that the writer's intention is to keep the robber's presence concealed from us as well as Eugene, a slug line to isolate EUGENE from the master shot of the store would restrict our view.

- The robber's voice would then be designated as (O.S.), so that we do not see him as he speaks to Eugene.

- Using the slug line EUGENE keeps him as the dominant object on-screen. The writer can now have the robber enter the store without being seen in the master shot.

But when the robber does become visible in the scene, the writer must use the RETURN TO SCENE slug line. Remember, when we do see the robber, he must be properly introduced by capping his character-name and giving him a brief description.

NEGLECTING CHARACTER EXITS

In the zeal of writing of scenes in which characters enter and exit, it is seldom a problem to write their entrances but it is often easy to overlook their exits.

- Remember that a character is always in the scene until the instructions call for an exit.

- When a character needs to leave a scene, you *must* write that into the instructions.

THE ORIGINAL VERSION:

```
The BUS BOY clears the table.

                    PETER
                 (delighted)
         Ah, that was wonderful.


                    KATHLEEN
         Ummm, I'm stuffed.  How about a walk
         along the river?

Peter signals for the bill.

Their Waiter appears at the table and hands the bill to Peter.
Peter takes the bill, smiles at Kathleen and hands the Waiter
a credit card.  The Waiter then returns to the table with the
receipt.
```

Track Characters Carefully

Although it may seem logical that characters enter and leave on their own, in a screenplay, you need to be specific. In this example, two characters enter but are not instructed to leave.

- The Bus Boy who clears the table will remain at the table until an instruction is added for him to leave.

  His departure is just as important as his arrival.

- The Waiter can't return to the table with the receipt because, according to the instructions, he never leaves the table after Peter hands him the credit card.

NOTE: ALLOW ENOUGH TIME FOR AN ACTION

Another problem with the preceding example is that it does not allow enough time for the Waiter to take the credit card, run it through the machine, and return it to Peter.

This can be easily corrected by shifting the dialogue and perhaps adding another dialogue exchange while the Waiter is away.

A CORRECTED VERSION:

```
The BUS BOY clears the table and leaves.

Peter signals for the bill.

Their Waiter appears at the table and hands the bill to Peter.
Peter takes the bill, smiles at Kathleen and hands it back to
the Waiter with a credit card.  The Waiter leaves.

                    PETER
                 (delighted)
            Ah, that was wonderful.


                    KATHLEEN
            Ummm, I'm stuffed.  How about a walk
            along the river?


                    PETER
            That would be perfect!


                    KATHLEEN
            We could watch the fireworks display
            from the bridge.

The Waiter returns with the credit card and receipt.
```

Dialogue-Block Mistakes

FORMATTING A SONG OR POEM IMPROPERLY

Song lyrics and poetry are not formatted in the same way as regular dialogue.

THE ORIGINAL VERSION:

```
LIVING ROOM

Susanna kneels down in front of her CD collection, excitedly
thumbing through the discs for something to play.  She smiles
as she finds a medley of Stephen Foster folk music.

Excitedly, she inserts the disc into the player and fumbles to
turn the stereo on.  She dashes into -

THE BEDROOM -

and runs up to the mirror, swaying back and forth.  The beat of
the SONG "Oh, Susanna" fills the room as she begins to dance.

                    SUSANNA
                (singing in unison)
        I come from Alabama with my banjo on my
        knee.  I'm goin' to Lou'siana my true
        love for to see.  It rained all night
        the day I left, the weather it was
        dry.  The sun so hot I froze to death,
        Susanna don't you cry.

RETURN TO SCENE

Susanna flops on the bed, exhausted.
```

Use a Special Format for Song Lyrics and Poetry

Although similar to the formatting for dialogue, song lyrics and poetry should be written in lines that simulate the way in which they would be sung or spoken.

A CORRECTED VERSION:

```
LIVING ROOM

Susanna kneels down in front of her CD collection, excitedly
thumbing through the discs for something to play.  She smiles
as she finds a medley of Stephen Foster folk music.

Excitedly, she inserts the disc into the player and fumbles to
turn the stereo on.  She dashes into -

THE BEDROOM -

and runs up to the mirror, swaying back and forth.  The beat of
the SONG "Oh, Susanna" fills the room as she begins to dance.
```

```
                        SUSANNA
                  (singing in unison)
      I come from Alabama with my banjo on my knee;
      I'm goin' to Lou'siana my true love for to see.
      It rained all night the day I left,
      the weather it was dry;
      The sun so hot I froze to death,
      Susanna don't you cry.

RETURN TO SCENE

At song's end, Susanna flops on the bed, exhausted.
```

CREATING UNWIELDY PARENTHETICALS

Both parentheticals and instructions provide information to the reader. However, you must be careful to note the different function that each serves.

THE ORIGINAL VERSION:

```
                        CAROL
                  (leaving the bed and heading
                  toward the vanity)
      Principally because that is something
      we have in common.

                        JORDAN
                  (shouting)
      And don't you care about my health?

                        CAROL
                  (screaming at him from the
                  vanity and starting to lose
                  control of herself as the phone
                  RINGS; both ignore the ringing)
      The great question is: Don't you care
      about mine?

                        JORDAN
                  (leaving the bed and facing
                  her back while Carol sits at
                  the vanity combing her hair)
      Calm down, will you?  You don't do
      anything all day long.
```

Use Parentheticals Only to Refer to Dialogue

Parentheticals and instructions have distinctly different applications. A *parenthetical* is a note to the *actor* about the dialogue that follows. Any description about what happens in the *scene* must be carried by the *instructions*.

- In this example, with the exception of Jordan "shouting" and Carol "screaming" (which are legitimate parentheticals), all the other pieces of information are more about the scene than how the dialogue is to be spoken.

- Further, all the parentheticals are too long and detailed. Such clutter impairs the flow of the narrative and detracts from the dialogue.

A CORRECTED VERSION:

```
Carol leaves the bed and heads toward the vanity.

                    CAROL
          Principally because that is something
          we have in common.

                    JORDAN
              (shouting)
          And don't you care about my health?

The phone RINGS.  Both ignore the ringing.

                    CAROL
              (screaming; starting to lose
              control)
          The great question is: Don't you care
          about mine?

Jordan leaves the bed, moving behind Carol as she combs
her hair.

                    JORDAN
          Calm down, will you?  You don't do
          anything all day long.
```

SUMMARIZING DIALOGUE

With only a couple of exceptions, dialogue that is to be spoken by the characters must be written into the screenplay.

THE ORIGINAL VERSION:

```
INT.  UPSCALE RESTAURANT - EVENING

It is a hectic time.  WAITERS and BUS BOYS are busily
attending to the many PATRONS.  In the center of the room, a
PIANIST is playing soft background music.

Ben and Adriana, dressed in evening attire, are at their table
beginning the main course.  They are talking about their plans
for the future--how much money they'll make on the real estate
sale and how excited they are about their daughter's wedding.
```

> The couple keep talking throughout their meal. The waiter comes over to ask about coffee, but they decline.

Write All Dialogue That Will Be Distinctly Heard by the Audience

You cannot *summarize* dialogue in the instructions.

- Unless the actors playing Ben and Adriana have been instructed to ad lib some light background conversation, the writer is obliged to include their dialogue.

  In this instance, the information specified in the instructions about their conversation is too detailed to be dismissed as an ad lib.

- If their dinner conversation is not essential to the development of the narrative, perhaps a more efficient way of writing the scene would be to skip past it by using a slug line, such as LATER.

A CORRECTED VERSION:

```
INT.   UPSCALE RESTAURANT - EVENING

It is a hectic time.  WAITERS and BUS BOYS are busily
attending to the many PATRONS.  In the center of the room, a
PIANIST is playing soft background music.

Ben and Adriana, dressed in evening attire, are at their
table beginning the main course.

                    ADRIANA
          So, how much do you think we'll make
          on the Talbot sale?  That land's
          right in the middle of the city's
          renovation project.

                    BEN
               (couldn't be happier)
          More than enough to retire and to pay
          cash for the most lavish wedding this
          town has seen!

LATER

They have finished their meal, and their plates are being
cleared by the Bus Boy.  The Waiter approaches.

                    WAITER
          Would you care for some coffee this
          evening?

Ben looks at Adriana who declines with a slight gesture.

                    BEN
          No, thank you.  Just the check,
          please, and make it quick.
```